We The People

A Data Ethics Playbook
for a Democratic Society

Kathy Rondon

Technics Publications

TECHNICS PUBLICATIONS

TECHNOLOGY / LEADERSHIP

115 Linda Vista
Sedona, AZ 86336 USA
https://www.TechnicsPub.com

Edited by Sadie Hoberman
Cover design by Lorena Molinari

First Printing 2022

Copyright © 2021 by Mary Kathryn Rondon

ISBN, print ed.   9781634627528
ISBN, Kindle ed. 9781634627535
ISBN, ePub ed.   9781634627542
ISBN, PDF ed.   9781634627559

Library of Congress Control Number: 2022943113

Acknowledgments

The journey toward publishing this book has been aided by several people over the years. Thanks to Peter Aiken, who has acted as a sounding board and provided encouragement to me on all things data. Thanks to Tony Shaw and his Dataversity team, who have allowed me a platform at various conferences to develop my narrative. Thanks to the folks who agreed to be interviewed for this book (they are called out with attribution throughout the text). And, finally, thanks to my husband Mark, who patiently listened to my stream of consciousness as I worked out issues I was writing about, even though he's not in any sense a data "nerd".

Contents

Introduction

In 2016, HBO premiered the series Westworld. Taking place in a not-too-distant future, the story follows a theme park of Artificial Intelligence (AI)-enabled robotic park "hosts." Many of the theme park human customers take the opportunity to do things they would not do in the "real world," and the ethical argument that takes place early on in the series is one of questioning where consciousness begins and whether depraved actions toward the "not human" are really depraved at all—or just letting off steam. By season three of Westworld, though, the real point has become apparent: that the theme park revenue was not the point at all, but rather the collection of enormous amounts of data about attendees, the aggregation of that data with other data from vast repositories, and the use of that data to control very real lives in the very real world. In a seminal scene in Westworld season three, a character, becoming aware of the scope of the data collection and its use society-wide says, "So, it tells them who I am?" The chilling response is, "It's not about who you are, Caleb. It's about who they'll let you become."

Dystopian? Maybe not. In 2020, The Washington Post reported on "surveillance scores" developed by data collection and analysis companies—who operate almost entirely without regulation—and how those scores can have dire consequences. The impact of credit rating companies like Equifax, TransUnion, and Experian are well-known but are only the tip of the iceberg.

CoreLogic, a California-based data analytics and business intelligence company, uses big data collection and analysis to provide scores to landlords to inform, not only the risk of a tenant not paying their rent on time, but also the ability of the tenant to absorb a rent increase. HireVue, a Utah-based company that provides a hiring software platform, also generates an "employability" score using large caches of proxy data on applicants.

Examples abound across the economy. These scores result in automated decisions that are not transparent to the scored subjects and that, in most cases, cannot be questioned or challenged.[1] This is a problem because data and its use are not, ipso facto, impartial and unbiased. And in a democratic society, the authoritarianism of "data" as inexorable undermines that democracy itself. Democratic societies need an ethical framework for data collection,

---

[1] "Data Isn't Just Being Collected From Your Phone. It's Being Used to Score You." Harvey Rosenfeld and Laura Antonini, The Washington Post, 31 July 2020. https://www.washingtonpost.com/opinions/2020/07/31/data-isnt-just-being-collected-your-phone-its-being-used-score-you/.

use, sharing, and retention—a framework that actively informs a society-wide legal and regulatory regime.

Where to look for an ethical framework

If you were to do a general internet search for the term "data ethics," you would find several different definitions and approaches. An article from the Harvard Business School online defines data ethics as "encompass[ing] the moral obligations of gathering, protecting, and using personally identifiable information and how it affects individuals."[2] Oxford University professor Luciano Floridi has defined data ethics as a branch of ethics that "studies and evaluates moral problems related to data…and corresponding practices…in order to formulate and support morally good solutions."[3] The Data Ethics Framework of the U.S. Government's Federal Data Strategy defines data ethics as, "norms of behavior that promote appropriate judgments and accountability when acquiring, managing, or using data, with the goals of

---

[2] "Five Principles of Data Ethics for Business." Catherine Cote, Harvard Business School Online, 16 March 2021. https://online.hbs.edu/blog/post/data-ethics.

[3] DOI: https://doi.org/10.1098/rsta.2016.3060.

protecting civil liberties, minimizing risks to individuals and society, and maximizing the public good."[4]

There are others, of course, but most suffer from the limitations of one or the other of these approaches. The first is too narrowly focused: exclusively on Personally Identifiable Information (PII) and the impact on or harm to a single individual (handling of PII is only part of what constitutes ethical conduct, as we shall see). The second is too broad: a purely macroethics approach that, while academically useful, does not help the data practitioner develop and adhere to a code of data ethics relevant to a specific context. The third is closer to an applied data ethics definition that both addresses context and is broad enough to encompass more than just handling of personally identifiable information. Still, it focuses on the activities of *government* data practitioners rather than other actors in a democratic society.

This book broadens the context of ethical conduct to not only focus on how democratic governments should conduct themselves in their own data activities, but also legislation and regulatory actions to be taken in establishing parameters for private entities in a democratic society. It further identifies quasi-public and private organizations in democratic societies that have outsized

---

[4] https://resources.data.gov/assets/documents/fds-data-ethics-framework.pdf.

roles to support—or undermine—the public good. Finally, this book includes suggestions on action items for individuals and organizations to consider in articulating and communicating the standards of ethical behavior in collecting, sharing, using, and retaining data.

This approach is more or less in line with the London-based Open Data Institute, which defines data ethics as, "a branch of ethics that evaluates data practices with the potential to adversely impact on people and society – in data collection, sharing and use."[5] The Open Data Institute (ODI) developed a Data Ethics Canvas consisting of types of questions to ask in conducting this ethical evaluation.[6]

The ODI foundational framework is, perhaps, the closest existing framework to the one discussed in this book. Readers looking at the Data Ethics Canvas in parallel with the questions raised in this book will notice some similarities. However, the ODI explicitly grounds its discussion in the UK and European context. While the ODI framework has a much further reach than just the UK and the European Union—and I hope this book will have a further reach than just the U.S. context—the differing approaches result in a fundamentally different discussion.

---

[5] https://theodi.org/article/the-data-ethics-canvas-2021/.

[6] Broad, Smith, and Wells, Helping Organizations Navigate Ethical Concerns in Their Data Practices, 2017.

And the case studies and advocacy suggestions in this book are specifically U.S.-focused.

So, how should we structure data ethics in a democratic society, using the United States as our specific example? We actually have some guidance on that score...

There is a whole generation of Americans who cannot say the Preamble to the U.S. Constitution—but we can sing it. I'm talking about my middle-aged cohort (some of us on the far side of middle-aged) who grew up on Saturday morning cartoons that included Schoolhouse Rock and the catchy tune that began "We the People...in order to form a more perfect union..." (Some of you now hear the whole song in your head—admit it.)

As I began conceptualizing this book on the ethical collection, retention, sharing, and use of data in a democratic society, I reflected on the aspirational goals of a democratic society in general.

Those aspirational goals articulated in the Preamble to the US Constitution do, in fact, lay out what we should be looking for as the data deluge threatens to overwhelm us.

We struggle to develop laws, policies, and regulations that allow the greatest freedom for the greatest number of people. At the same time, and this is very important, we need to mitigate as much as possible the great harms that can be done to individuals, large populations, and society as a whole when unfettered freedom is the only goal prioritized. Therefore, I structured this book according to the aspirational goals of the Preamble to the U.S. Constitution.

First, we will discuss what "we the people" means in the context of a foundation for data ethics in a democratic society. Chapter two examines how data collection, sharing, and use can advance a "more perfect union." In chapter three, we will discuss how data can "establish justice" and how, too often, using data and AI trained on inappropriate and biased data sets has led to injustice. In chapter four, we will explore the concept of "domestic tranquility," a goal that seems, as I write this, further away than it has been, at least, in my memory. Chapter five will look at the collection, sharing, and use of data to "provide for the common defense," a particularly interesting area for data ethics, given that transparency is not always possible in this environment—even in a democratic society. The goal of structuring our collection, sharing, retention, and use of data to "promote the general welfare" is the subject of chapter six. Finally, we will discuss what it means to view data through the lens of "secur[ing] the blessings of liberty to ourselves and our posterity."

Each section contains ethical questions, but these questions are not meant to be exhaustive. I have no doubt you will come up with additional ones. However, the format is intended to emphasize one of the overall points of this book: that the practice of data ethics is as much about asking the right questions—and asking them honestly, not as an exercise intended to "end run" compliance requirements—as it is the answer at the end of the process.

Ethics, law, and policy

You will notice discussions of law and policy throughout this book, in addition to ethics. All three are pillars in the development of normative behavior, and it would be an incomplete discussion of ethics without considering all three. As former U.S. Supreme Court Justice Potter Stewart once noted, "Ethics is knowing the difference between what you have a right to do and what is right to do."[7] Adding data policy to this equation starts to examine how we should do those actions.

It seems intuitive to think of the trajectory of behavioral norms leading from the law (what can I do?) to ethics (what should I do?) to policy (how do I do it?). But there is currently an identifiable void in the legal sphere in the collection, sharing, use, and retention of vast amounts of data.

----

[7] https://www.brainyquote.com/quotes/potter_stewart_390058.

What laws do exist are a patchwork of vague and often contradictory laws at the federal and state levels, supplemented with federal Executive Branch regulations. Despite the recent introduction from the U.S. House of Representatives of the draft "American Data Privacy and Protection Act," we are still a long way from a legal regime that addresses the potential harms and maximizes the potential public good of big data in a democratic society. This is not surprising, as technological advancements almost always outrun legal parameters for their use.

Ethical frameworks that apply to specific use cases of big data try to address the most egregious missteps of government and industry, such as AI development, the collection and use of student data, and the sale of consumer data. These ethical frameworks, though, have the weakness of being developed with the primary goal of preserving the status quo to the greatest extent possible. There is little incentive, particularly from a business standpoint, to be forward-leaning in protecting data rights of individuals when it negatively impacts the bottom line.

Therefore, the approach we will take is that, at this point in the societal data ethics discussion, law and ethics should form a feedback loop, with developing ethical frameworks informing the law, and legislative bodies seeking, not just to reflect ethical norms, but also to actively influence them toward a consistent basic standard that protects and supports individual rights, as well as overall business and civic interests. Based on that approach, throughout this book, you will find suggestions on advocating for new or improved legal requirements, constructing better ethical frameworks, and drafting policies that better address both. Like the ethical questions included in each chapter, these advocacy suggestions should not be considered exhaustive, but rather examples. I encourage you to use them as stepping off points for crafting your own advocacy for ethical data practices.

A few disclaimers

Before continuing, it is worth noting that, despite the reliance on the original text of the Preamble for its conceptual framework, this book is not an "originalist" work from a philosophical standpoint. The drafters of the Preamble (and the Constitution it introduces) were not particularly enamored of pure democracy, to be frank. Many of them considered it akin to mob rule. But they clearly did intend it to be aspirational, and it is in this vein—aspirations toward evolving democratic institutions—that this book is grounded.

Applying the Preamble to a data ethics discussion in a democratic society is intended to be aspirational and actionable. It also means that this book is very much "en medias res," so that by the time readers actually engage with this text, the discipline of data ethics may have evolved in ways that are either recommended by this narrative or in ways entirely unanticipated. Such is the risk of writing about an ongoing conversation.

A few additional disclaimers on what this book is not. Since this is a conceptual framework, those looking for a tool or a checklist for "ethical compliance" need to read no further. You won't find one here. This book, hopefully, will get the reader thinking about why they collect data in the first place, for what purpose, if that purpose is consistent with ethical goals in a democratic society, and, if there are downstream uses and sharing of data, whether ethical mitigation strategies are warranted. While this is not at all meant to be a political work, it would be disingenuous to think there are not political ramifications to the identification of places where we are clearly falling short of the aspirations articulated in the Preamble.

Also, I am not a "techie." My degrees are in English Literature and International Affairs, and my data governance and ethics work derive from my long-time work on drafting and negotiating policy associated with the collection and use of data in a public sector environment, as well as my work in developing training on those topics. There will be no content here on how to code or automate ethics rules into your data governance practice. In fact, it is my firm belief that trying to automate ethics misses the point of what ethics is all about.

Finally, I have spent the bulk of my career working in or alongside the federal government—as a government employee, a government contractor, and a business executive—so many of my examples will seem DC- or federal government-centric. I draw from what I know. The examples are, I hope, applicable to other situations and environments, however.

I hope you enjoy the journey and that this book starts a conversation that leads to ideas in your own specific situation on how data could be better leveraged toward a "more perfect union."

CHAPTER 1

We The People

Democracy is a process, not a static condition. It is becoming, rather than being. It can be easily lost, but is never finally won.

William H. Hastie
First Black federal judge in the United States
(appointed in 1937)

Who do we mean when we talk about "the people" in the context of data ethics in a democratic society? Who is included in "we the people" has changed and evolved over time...almost always toward being more (not less) inclusive in its definition. When the Preamble was written, full citizenship and civil rights in the United States were not typically granted to Black people (especially not those in a state of slavery), women, Native Americans, or Chinese laborers. Over time—and after a horrendous civil war, a suffrage movement, and a civil rights movement— more and more people have been included in an ever-expanding definition of "we the people."

That said, here is a first salvo in the discussion of "we the people" in the context of data ethics that may be controversial and rub some people the wrong way:

For the purposes of data ethics, a corporation is not a person.

Yes, yes. Judicial cases in the United States have upheld the "personhood" of corporations and associated rights—specifically freedom of speech—therein. And in the sense of ethical standards, as they apply to the collection and use of data, corporations have an outsized role to play.

The main point from a data ethics standpoint that argues against including corporations in the definition of "we the people" is that ethics have actors and those acted upon. Medical ethics applies to medical practitioners as they provide medical attention to patients, for example. In data ethics in a democratic society, corporations are overwhelmingly those who are actors, not the acted upon. So, the data ethics approaches discussed in this book should apply to government entities (at all levels of government) *and* corporations in democratic societies as they collect, share, use, and retain data on individual persons, defined groups of people, and entities and events that impact society.

This is not to say that the specific norms and standards that apply to government entities should also uniformly apply to corporations. After all, corporations generally form for profit, not solely for the public good, and those differing goals should be considered. But just as certain racial and gender-based discrimination policies by private entities are now illegal (a lunch counter can no longer refuse to seat a person based on race by claiming it is a private company and therefore can do as it likes), the evolving definition of "we the people" in a data ethics context requires an evolution in what private companies in a democratic society can do with data they collect...and what they cannot.

Who and what do we count and why?

As we consider the application of data ethics in a democratic society, it is useful to look at some examples of where lines have been drawn—and where those lines are still pretty fuzzy.

It is generally accepted that democratic societies are built upon twin pillars of majority rule and protection of minority and individual rights.[8] Laws and the courts exist to mediate those rights. However, neither laws nor the

---

[8] https://www.principlesofdemocracy.org.

courts have caught up to the ethical issues caused by collecting, sharing, and using large amounts of data.

Even when individuals and populations of people have data rights in a democratic society, data collecting, sharing, using, and retaining do not always reflect those rights. To be clear, it is not being suggested here that those making decisions based upon collected datasets would intentionally leave out or discount a segment of the population—whether that be women, people of color, the disabled, the elderly, children, or any population considered "other." Yet the dominant perspective tends to assume that its perspective is universally applicable. This is not usually with malicious intent, but it nevertheless results in inequitable outcomes.

Action Item

— Better Ethical Framework —

Being "data-driven" is a stated goal of most data governance and data management programs in both public and private sectors. But is it ethical to be "data-driven" if you know or suspect your data is incomplete or biased? Or if you assume your data is unbiased and make decisions on it without actively confirming this assumption? Organizations should review their ethical codes of conduct to ensure that they include steps to review data for bias and articulate caveats for decision-makers relying on data and derived data products.

For example, in most plumbing codes for public buildings, there is a 50/50 division of floor space between men's and women's restrooms. This might seem fair. However, as any woman at any public event will tell you, it is certainly not equitable. That is because floor space is not used equally. Between urinals and stalls, men's restrooms can accommodate many more concurrent users than women's restrooms. In addition, women typically take roughly twice as long to use a restroom as men for a variety of reasons: women are more likely to be caregivers of children and elderly who need help using a restroom; they are eight times as likely to suffer from urinary tract infections; and roughly one-quarter of women of childbearing age will have their period at any given time.[9]

In other words, data that is used for decision-making and, more to the point, data that is NOT used for decision-making, can have a definite impact on people's lives. In a democratic society, considering these impacts is a very relevant ethical question.

Let's look at some examples of how the definition and focus of "we the people" in data collection and use can

---

[9] Caroline Credo Perez, Invisible Women: Data Bias in a World Designed for Men, 2019, ISBN: 978-1-4197-2907-2.

lead to less than optimal outcomes, either intentionally or unintentionally.

It is generally acknowledged in both legislation and judicial precedent in the United States that even those without citizenship rights still are allowed human, legal, and civil rights in our democratic society. One of the most controversial applications of this "we the people" definition as it applies to the collection and use of data on persons is undocumented immigrants. Indeed, this population was chosen for this example precisely because it sits squarely in the middle of an ongoing debate of the definition of "we the people."

While trying not to take political sides in an admittedly heated debate on U.S. immigration policy, we can still try to discern a reasonable data ethics approach to these questions: What are the ethical considerations in collecting and using data on undocumented immigrants, and are those considerations different for this defined group than for documented immigrants or citizens in a democratic society? There are two separate ethical issues inherent in this question:

1. Is it ethical to collect personally identifiable information on undocumented immigrants in ways that would not be allowed for citizens and documented immigrants?

2. Does using collected data in ways that purposely include or dismiss data on undocumented immigrants skew analytical results in a manner that does not meet ethical standards?

First, let's consider the collection of data on undocumented immigrants in ways that would not be allowed for citizens or documented immigrants. There is actually a possible counterfactual to this question. Without collecting official citizenship or visa documentation data on everyone, how do you know who is undocumented? Efforts to do this often rely on proxy data that instantly slides into racial or ethnic profiling.

As a thought experiment, consider collecting data on the unhoused population in any given city. How many members of this population could produce a birth certificate or a passport? Probably not many. Would it be ethical from a collection standpoint to assume that a White native English speaker was here legally, but that a non-White Spanish speaker was not, when neither could produce documentation one way or the other? We can then stipulate that collecting data on undocumented immigrants may pose ethical problems in terms of both profiling and analytical integrity, unless we uniformly collect documentation from all members of the stipulated population. In the absence of such a documentation requirement, statistical models that estimate a population of undocumented immigrants based upon proxy data have an inherent margin of error.

In addition to the statistical margins for error, there is also the issue of post hoc analysis of data. Publication ethics standards associated with the use of proxy data and post-hoc analysis require that such post hoc analysis be specifically identified and all issues of bias be considered and mitigated. Failure to do so renders the analytical results unreliable.[10]

So, leaving aside political issues and viewpoints, we can reasonably say that the collection of data on undocumented immigrants from a data ethics standpoint either needs to be consistent with data collected from all members of the total population regardless of documentation status, or the use of proxy data identified, rigorously reviewed for bias, and margins for error calculated and made transparent to end users.

What if such documentation IS required and undocumented immigrants can be more or less reliably identified in the population, or bias mitigation and margins for error have been considered, established, and communicated? Are there ethical considerations in how the analyst uses that data?

---

[10] Committee on Publication Ethics. https://publicationethics.org/.

To answer this question, data ethics in a democratic society requires consideration of "common good" or "public good" arguments. As the Federal Data Strategy Ethics Framework points out, a large component of ethical norms of government data collection and use is "maximizing the public good." This admonition can be problematic since, in a pluralistic democratic society, what constitutes "the public good" is a matter of intense debate and tends to evolve over time. Therefore, it is clear we are not looking for an answer, here, but rather the right questions to ask. Taking our undocumented immigrant example, let's see if we can discern the right questions to ask in the use of data once it is collected.

In January of 2021, the director of the U.S. Census Bureau resigned in the wake of allegations that he had supported a partisan push to deliver data on undocumented immigrants resulting from the 2020 census. In particular, whistleblower complaints alleged that political appointees were pressuring staff members to release state tallies of undocumented immigrants by January 15th, regardless of their accuracy, to boost efforts to exclude them from congressional apportionment. The Census Director, in replying to the accusation, said that he "was informed that the data review and any potential publication of *summary numbers or estimates* would comply with quality standards used by the Bureau in producing 'technical reports.' "[11] But, by law, congressional apportionment requires a higher standard than technical reports, and must be based on *actual numbers, not estimates.* If this action had been carried out, and congressional apportionment had excluded estimated numbers of undocumented immigrants, the impact would have fallen equally on U.S. citizens and legal permanent residents, as states with high estimated numbers of undocumented immigrants may well have lost congressional seats and federal funding— which could not possibly have been tailored to impact only the undocumented.

There are other examples of ethical questions associated with using data when there is a question of whether it would be appropriate to do so from an analytical perspective. In late 2021, advocates for immigration reform in Congress collected and presented data on the economic impacts of undocumented immigration in a play to pass immigration reform as part of budget reconciliation. (The budget reconciliation process bypasses the filibuster and allows passage in Congress using a simple majority, but it is limited to budgetary concerns.) Senate parliamentarian

---

[11] *"Census Director Resigns,"* Tara Bahrampour, Washington Post, 18 January 2021. https://www.washingtonpost.com/local/social-issues/embattled-census-bureau-director-steven-dillingham-resigns/2021/01/18/63c8d1aa-59bb-11eb-a976-bad6431e03e2_story.html.

Elizabeth MacDonough's response was something along the lines of, "nice try, but no." Stretching the definition of budgetary data to include anything that could arguably have an economic impact was a bridge too far.[12]

What are the ethical questions?

In both the above cases, the definition of "we the people" and the concept of "public good" were open to political interpretation. One might argue that undocumented immigrants should be excluded, as a matter of public good, from congressional apportionment, but that is not necessarily relevant to the data ethics question. One might also argue that immigration reform is necessary to achieve public good, but that also is not necessarily relevant to the data ethics question. So, in examining the concept of "we the people," what are the data ethics questions to be asked (and which can be extrapolated to other cases, regardless of the political definition of public good)?

- What is the articulated public good served by the inclusion or exclusion of data about a subgroup?

---

[12] *"Senate Parliamentarian Rejects Immigration Reform in Democrats' Spending Bill,"* Claudia Grisales, National Public Radio, 16 December 2021. https://www.npr.org/2021/12/16/1061030363/senate-parliamentarian-rejects-immigration-reform-in-democrats-spending-bill.

- Is the inclusion or exclusion of subgroup data transparent to those making policy decisions or taking action based on the data?

- Are there negative implications to a subgroup of the inclusion or omission of data? Note: negative implications to a group do not necessarily make the inclusion or use of data unethical. However, actively considering implications and making them transparent is appropriate for ethical data use in a democratic society and helps decision-makers understand and mitigate negative consequences.

- Are there negative implications to the inclusion or omission of data about a subgroup to the population as a whole (not only the subgroup)?

- Is there accountable oversight of the decision to include or exclude subgroup data?

- Does the inclusion or exclusion of subgroup data follow established quality parameters and stated data analytical processes and adhere to all applicable legal and regulatory requirements? If exceptions are to be made to policy, processes, or quality standards (exceptions to legal requirements are not an option), then that exception must be explicitly noted, explained, and justified.

These questions should be asked as a matter of course when including or excluding data about a defined group of people. Trying to end run any of these questions or ask the questions a different way or to a different person simply to get the answer one wants (for a political or any other reason) would constitute unethical data practices.

CHAPTER 2

In Order to Form a More Perfect Union

*If the men and women of the past, with all their flaws and
limitations and ambitions and appetites, could press on
through ignorance and superstition, racism and sexism,
selfishness and greed, to create a freer, stronger nation, then
perhaps we, too, can right wrongs and take another step
toward that most enchanting and elusive destination: a more
perfect Union.*

Jon Meacham
Author, historian, and presidential biographer, 2018

Historians and legal scholars have construed the phrase in
the Preamble "to form a more perfect Union" as literally
referring to the shift to the Constitution from the Articles
of Confederation. A more perfect union need not stop
there, though. If it did, this country and society would be
pretty stagnant. There are multiple examples in which
laws and courts have raised the bar on a more perfect
union in these United States. For example, shortly after the
Civil War and the ratification of the Fourteenth

Amendment, the Supreme Court said that the "Union" was made "more perfect" by the creation of a federal government with enough power to act directly upon citizens, rather than a government with narrowly limited power that could act on citizens only indirectly through the states, e.g., by imposing taxes (Lane County v. Oregon). While this balance between federal and state prerogatives is, as of mid-2022, again a matter of heated political discussion, the idea of evolution of the "union" is clearly one that has deep historical roots.

In the 21st century, a widely reported speech entitled "A More Perfect Union" by then-candidate Barack Obama in 2008, defined "a more perfect union" in the context of moving beyond racial tensions and embracing opportunity for all. Specifically, he noted that "It is not enough to give health care to the sick, or jobs to the jobless, or education to our children. But it is where we start. It is where our union grows stronger. And as so many generations have come to realize over the course of the two-hundred and twenty-one years since a band of patriots signed that document in Philadelphia, that is where the perfection begins."[13]

The collection, sharing, use, and retention of data can certainly support or hinder such a goal. In subsequent chapters, we will discuss data ethics in the context of racial

---

[13] https://www.americanrhetoric.com/speeches/barackobamaperfectunion.htm.

equity in more detail. In this chapter, we will focus on expanding the notion of a more perfect union as it applies to data ethics in terms of three foundational goals: transparency, privacy, and accountability.

Transparency

In pondering transparency and data ethics in a democratic society, consider that a democracy, by definition, exercises governing power either directly or indirectly through the governed.

This might sound pedantic, but it has real implications to implementing data ethics in a democratic society. It means that the governed must be sufficiently informed of government operation to provide input.

The ethical collection, sharing, use, and retention of data in such an environment should include mechanisms to disseminate such information as widely as possible and in a manner that the greatest majority of the population can understand and use. There are, of course, exceptions to data and information disclosure, even in a democratic society. We will discuss some such exceptions in Chapter Five (Provide for the Common Defense). Leaving aside exceptions, for now, let's look at transparency in data collection, sharing, use, and retention by considering freedom of information laws. This is a particularly useful data ethics case study because it highlights ethical considerations that often have nothing to do with the collection and use of personally identifiable information (PII), demonstrating how ethics frameworks that focus only on PII are insufficient to address data ethics in a democratic society.

The concept of transparency in this context refers principally to the right of citizens and residents to have access to data about the operations of their government. In the United States, this right is codified in the Freedom of Information Act. The basic function of the Freedom of Information Act (FOIA) is "...to ensure informed citizens, vital to the functioning of a democratic society. The FOIA provides that government agencies should withhold information only if they reasonably foresee that disclosure would harm an interest protected by an exemption, or if disclosure is prohibited by law."[14]

While FOIA applies to federal government agencies in the United States, there are parallel versions of FOIA at the state level and even at municipal levels. And many democratic nations across the globe have a version of a freedom of information law, the oldest being Sweden's Freedom of the Press Act, originally passed in 1766 and

---

[14] FOIA.gov.

updated in 1949. So, there is a long-standing tradition of requests for information and responses to those requests that pre-date the digital era.

When it works as intended, right-to-information laws hold the government accountable to the governed and other power players accountable to both. Examples of how this has played out in the United States are many and varied, and it is often investigative journalists who do most of the work to collect and review information from records requests and then make that information available to the general public easily in an understandable format.

For example, in 2017, USA Today journalists used freedom of information requests to obtain and assess labor dispute records in their investigative series "Rigged: Forced into debt. Worked past exhaustion. Left with nothing." an investigative report on the exploitation of truckers.[15] In 2017-2018, FOIA requests for records from the Environmental Protection Agency (EPA) from nonprofits and journalists formed the basis for news stories alleging

---

[15] *"Rigged: Forced into debt. Worked past exhaustion. Left with nothing."* Brett Murphy, USA Today, 16 June, 2017.
https://www.usatoday.com/pages/interactives/news/rigged-forced-into-debt-worked-past-exhaustion-left-with-nothing/.

the misuse of government funds by the director of the EPA, leading to his eventual resignation.[16]

However, the explosion of digital data has complicated a process that is still largely analog and manual, resulting in an ethical problem for government agencies trying to respond to such requests. These agencies don't always intend to limit transparency, but limited it has become, nonetheless. Consider the case of the U.S. Food and Drug Administration (FDA). A FOIA request filed by Public Health and Medical Professionals for Transparency in the midst of the global COVID pandemic requested essentially all information the FDA had on the Pfizer COVID vaccine, including correspondence, clinical trial data, and manufacturing data. The FDA responded in November 2021, proposing to release thousands of "high priority" pages at the beginning of 2022, and then slowing the pace to 500 pages per month thereafter. While the proposed response was in line with the FDA's policies and standards based on its legacy data collection and storage systems, the full response to the FOIA request would take…55 years.

Indeed, more routine FOIA requests to FDA often take years to complete. This is partly the result of a need to

---

[16] "Ex-Aide Says He'll Take Credit for Pruitt's Downfall." Miranda Greene, The Hill, 8 July 2018. https://thehill.com/policy/energy-environment/396000-ex-aide-says-hell-take-credit-for-pruitts-downfall/.

protect proprietary data (which is a FOIA exemption, by the way) of drug manufacturers, and self-imposed FDA disclosure rules that make the process of reviewing information for disclosure highly manual and painstaking. Both Congress and the Federal Courts have weighed in on the side of requesters instructing the FDA to be more forthcoming with information, but FOIA is already a heavy financial burden on the agency, costing over $300 million between 2008 and 2017.[17]

Action Item

— Better Policy —

Proprietary information is an exemption to the federal Freedom of Information Act and most other laws at the state and municipal level, but the use of this exemption could be better implemented. Updated policies at government agencies should list <u>specific justifications allowed for the use of the "proprietary" label</u>, and the onus should be on data providers to justify and mark such information in advance. This could speed up the review process and make it easier to automate.

If you work at a government agency, try advocating for better implementation of the "proprietary" exemption. As a citizen advocate, write your government representatives to encourage better definition of proprietary labels in freedom of information laws.

---

[17] Morten, et.al., The Washington Post, 19 December 2021.

Does the FDA have an ethical responsibility to provide more data on a more aggressive time scale to meet transparency requirements in a democratic society? If so, how should it? And how should other government agencies, as the FDA is not the only one with such a conundrum, approach FOIA requests in the new digital era?

I would argue the answer to the first question is yes. The FDA and other government agencies have an ethical responsibility to disseminate information on their operations that impact the public good. The default should be to interpret "public good" as broadly as possible. In other words, the tendency should be toward, and not away from, transparency. To take any other approach risks the collection, sharing, use, and retention of data being conducted in the shadows, which is an ethical problem in and of itself in a democratic society, and risks leading to more active unethical actions, as the light of oversight becomes dim.

Protection of proprietary information is important and should not be taken lightly, but the onus should be on the corporation to proactively identify, justify, and mark proprietary information. If such information is not proactively identified, justified, and marked, then it should not be considered exempt from FOIA release under this exemption; another manual review should not be required.

The answer to the second question is more complex: how to address the problem. FOIA backlogs at many agencies are often so long that they border on simple non-responsiveness. How can this be addressed with the goal of more transparency and more ethical treatment of data collected for the public good? More money is an easy answer, but not the right one since simply increasing the funding for antiquated processes and policies that will continue to "not scale" is rarely the answer. The global pandemic of 2020-2021 put a blinding spotlight on this issue.

In October 2020, The Washington Post reported that already large FOIA backlogs before the pandemic became complete halts on FOIA responses of any kind in some agencies several months into the pandemic. A Congressional Research Service report noted that the multiple physical and digital systems needed to process FOIA requests made employees' tasks especially difficult, and that access to information and systems that held requested records could not be made remotely. Eric Stein, head of the State Department's FOIA program, said in response to a FOIA lawsuit, that his agency employs retired Foreign Service Officers to process requests manually. Stein said: "The vast majority of [these officials] are not telework ready."[18]

The reality is that this network of anachronistic processes and policies across the federal government was already hearing its death knell—the pandemic simply made it impossible to ignore. Bringing ethical practices back in line with the transparency that the law was designed to promote, relies on changes in mindset, culture, policy, and law.

Unfortunately, governments sometimes intend to limit transparency despite, or even in the direct face of, right-to-information laws. This is a more overt ethical issue: when government entities use the letter of the law to end run the spirit of the law.

One such example can be found in the Commonwealth of Virginia, where successive administrations of both parties have used an exemption in the state's right to information law for Office of the Governor "working papers and correspondence" to avoid releasing anything the Governor's Office simply doesn't want to release. The

---

[18] *"Public Records requests fall Victim to the Coronavirus Pandemic."* Nate Jones, The Washington Post, 1 October 2020.
https://www.washingtonpost.com/investigations/public-records-requests-fall-victim-to-the-coronavirus-pandemic/2020/10/01/cba2500c-b7a5-11ea-a8da-693df3d7674a_story.html.

more current example is Governor Glenn Youngkin's refusal to release information about a tip line set up for people to report possible violations of his Executive Order prohibiting the teaching of "inherently divisive concepts" in public schools. I, myself, put in a records request for this information to have it wholly refused under the "working papers" exemption. I was not the only one, however. As of April 2022, over a dozen news organizations had filed a lawsuit against the Youngkin administration for refusing to release the same information.[19]

Action Item

— Better Legislation —

State and municipal level freedom of information laws should have narrowly focused and well-defined exemptions, not broad "anything you want to exempt" loopholes. As a citizen advocate, review your state or city's freedom of information law. If it has broad exemptions, write your representative or city council and ask that the law be updated or amended.

It would be remiss not to mention that the previous administration of Virginia Governor Ralph Northam also found it convenient to answer a difficult request with the

---

[19] *"News Organizations Sue Youngkin Over School Tip Line Emails."* Denise Lavoie, Associated Press, 22 April 2022.
https://www.13newsnow.com/article/news/local/virginia/news-youngkin-foia-lawsuit-emails/291-4f9b747a-5bf6-42db-bf18-96135ef7a435.

"working papers" exemption when an environmental group requested his daily calendar of meetings (specifically with utility executives) in advance of key pipeline legislation.[20]

Freedom of information laws are not designed to protect elected officials from the inconveniences of their policy choices. This is where it becomes apparent that legal compliance and ethical behavior are not synonymous and that a code of data ethics is required in a democratic society—not just a legal data compliance team.

Privacy

The whole concept of a legal right to privacy has been hotly debated for several decades, but data privacy is a newer concept and, from a legal standpoint, murky at best. The "right to privacy" legal concept was famously articulated in the seminal Samuel Warren and Louis Brandeis Harvard Law Review article in 1890, in the face of that emerging disruptive technology, the photograph. In their article, Warren and Brandeis reiterated the common

---

[20] *"Working Papers Exemption Claimed to Shield Governor's Calendar Amid Pipeline Permit Uproar."* Mechelle Hankerson, Virginia Mercury, 28 November 2018. https://www.virginiamercury.com/2018/11/28/working-papers-exemption-claimed-to-shield-governors-calendar-amid-pipeline-permit-uproar/.

law bar that a party had to show "harm," but that such harm did not have to be bodily, monetary, or even reputational, but could rather be based on "the general right of the individual to be let alone."[21] But that was in 1890, when the specific subject and recipient of personal information could easily be determined, and the method of dissemination transparent.

Fast forward more than 100 years, and things are quite a bit more complicated. Recent scholarly work on this topic in a big data environment has pointed out that "When privacy violations result in negative consequences, the effects are often small – frustration, aggravation, anxiety, inconvenience – and dispersed among a large number of people. When these minor harms are suffered at a vast scale, they produce significant harm to individuals, groups, and society. But these harms do not fit well with existing cramped judicial understandings of harm."[22]

One of the looming questions of ethical collection, sharing, use, and retention of personally identifiable data in a

---

[21] "The Right to Privacy." Samuel Warren and Louis Brandeis, Harvard Law Review, 15 December 1890. https://www.cs.cornell.edu › warren-brandeis.

[22] Citron, Danielle Keats and Solove, Daniel J., *Privacy Harms*, February 9, 2021; GWU Legal Studies Research Paper No. 2021-11, GWU Law School Public Law Research Paper No. 2021-11, Boston University Law Review, Vol. 102, 2022, Available at SSRN: https://ssrn.com/abstract=3782222 or http://dx.doi.org/10.2139/ssrn.3782222).

democratic society is this question of protection of individual and minority rights as it applies to identifying information about oneself. A growing body of legal commentary has focused on Fourth Amendment protections of one's genetic information—as in the 2018 case of the Golden State Killer, who was tracked down using DNA of family members on genealogy websites.[23] But this deals with the *government*'s collection and use of data, which we will dive deeper into that question in a subsequent chapter. In the United States today, the vast majority of issues surrounding the "right of the people to be secure in their persons" are taking place in the private sector, with a largely unregulated and opaque collection and sale of data for whatever purpose the collector and purchaser desires. Let's look at one such loophole as it concerns data privacy regarding health data. People in the United States typically assume that any data about their health is protected under The Health Insurance Portability and Accountability Act (HIPAA). HIPAA is actually fairly narrow, and only governs data held by specified "covered entities." The problem is that the medical world has evolved since HIPAA was passed in 1996, and the definition of covered entities is woefully outdated.

---

[23] *"The Golden State Killer and Genetic Privacy."* Erin Murphy, Andrea Roth, and Jeffrey Rosen, We The People Podcast, 21 June 2018.
https://constitutioncenter.org/interactive-constitution/podcast/the-golden-state-killer-and-genetic-privacy.

HIPAA does not, for example, cover the previously unknown but now ubiquitous patient portals that a majority of patients now use to update and manage their consumption of healthcare services. These portals are *not* "covered entities" under HIPAA. Instead, Business Associate Agreements govern the collection and use of the data, which vary widely and are not subject to HIPAA sanctions for breach or misuse. Patients are typically not informed that these portals are not HIPAA-covered entities. Indeed, many healthcare providers are surprised to learn this is the case. Also, there is no transparency as to exactly what is included in the Business Associate Agreements between the portal provider and the healthcare provider. Try asking your healthcare provider for a copy, if you don't believe it.

The press has reported this issue. For example, Geoffrey Fowler, a technology columnist for The Washington Post, wrote about a reader who, surprisingly, found that her portal account with her doctor had a policy that "reserved the right" to use her data for marketing.[24]

---

[24] "Help Desk: Can Your Medical Records Become Marketing?" Geoffrey Fowler, The Washington Post, 22 October 2019.
https://www.washingtonpost.com/technology/2019/10/22/help-desk-can-your-medical-records-become-marketing-we-investigate-readers-suspicious-patient-portal/.

I have also done sleuthing on my own, writing to my healthcare provider about their practice's portal account. (As a contextual note, the practice is affiliated with a large hospital, so they had a substantial legal, policy, and privacy team to consult.) Unfortunately, most people have neither the time nor motivation to track down answers to these questions and to push when unsatisfactory answers are initially provided. So that you don't have to suffer the annoyance, here's a summary of how my own conversation went:

- I asked for a copy of the data privacy and data sharing agreement between the healthcare provider and the platform provider. I noted that the privacy policy available through the system provided information about how the <u>healthcare provider</u> would keep data private. There was not, however, any information about how the <u>platform provider</u> could access or use or share my data on their system.

- The provider responded that the platform could only use personal health information (PHI) in accordance with HIPAA regulations per their Business Associate Agreement.

- I responded with a more narrowly worded question as to whether the Business Associate Agreement noted that the platform provider was also a covered entity and had the SAME HIPAA restrictions as the provider. I noted my concern that other platforms have argued that their Business Associate Agreement does not make them a covered entity. So, the same HIPAA restrictions that apply to the health provider do not apply to them. In other words, <u>because</u> they are not a HIPAA-covered entity, they could conceivably use the data to target ads for health services, for example, and still be HIPAA-compliant. I specifically asked to see the language in the Business Associate Agreement.

- The provider then responded that the platform provider was NOT a covered entity. They said the definition of a covered entity per HIPAA includes Health Plans, Health Care Clearing Houses, and Health Care Providers. The electronic record-keeping platform provider was none of these types of organizations. They further noted that it was my right to choose to opt out of using the portal, and that the healthcare provider's Notice of Privacy Practices informs patients (somewhere—I never actually found the language) "that they can opt out of the use of their information for marketing and fund raising."

- I responded, "YES PLEASE," I would like to opt out of using my data for marketing and fundraising. I further told the healthcare provider that OPT OUT should be the default and that they should ask patients to OPT IN.

- After yet another attempt at getting a copy of the Business Associate Agreement, I was told this agreement was considered proprietary information and could not be shared with patients. But the essence of the issue is that when you sign up for a portal account, it is no accident that a link is sent to you to sign up. It is not your doctor (who is a covered entity) creating the account for you. When you create your account, it is <u>you</u>, the individual, who is the customer and putting data voluntarily on the portal. And neither you nor the portal provider is a HIPAA-covered entity.

Action Item

— Better Legislation —

An update is needed to the Health Insurance Portability and Accountability Act (HIPAA) to close the loophole that leaves electronic patient portals and telemedicine applications out of the list of "covered entities." What can you do? Write your congresspersons and ask that they support an update to HIPAA.

Not only electronic record-keeping portals fall into this "platform" loophole. Mental health telehealth platforms exploded during the pandemic, and there is no reason to believe they will go away after the COVID-19 pandemic. These applications allow a patient to connect virtually with a licensed mental health professional for therapy, diagnoses, and even prescription medication. The mental health providers are HIPAA-covered entities. The patient records <u>in their possession</u> are covered under HIPAA. The company providing the application, however? Not so much. Again, if you Google mental health applications and HIPAA, you will find all sorts of assurances that they are "HIPAA-compliant," but just like the patient records portals, this is misleading. If the platform is not a HIPAA-covered entity, then "HIPAA-compliance" does not carry many restrictions on data collection and use.

In July 2022, the U.S. Senate directly questioned popular mental health telemedicine apps about their data collection, sharing, and storage practices.[25] And whereas electronic patient portals are at least subject to Business Associate Agreements (even though patients have no visibility into these agreements), mental health app developers generally aren't even subject to these parameters. In 2021, Consumer Reports Digital Lab conducted a study of the seven most popular mental health applications and found numerous documented leaks of mental health information, including intentional

---

[25] *"Senators Question Mental Health App Providers About Privacy and Data Sharing Practices."* HIPAA Journal, 1 July 2022. https://www.hipaajournal.com/senators-question-mental-health-app-providers-questioned-about-privacy-and-data-sharing-practices/.

sharing of data with Facebook.[26] Some application providers said they were updating their privacy policies (in direct response to the Consumer Reports study), but this is at the company's discretion, can be changed at any time, and is almost certainly designed to preserve the company's bottom line over any other consideration. They are, after all, for-profit entities with no regulatory requirement to do otherwise.

The moral of this story? Let me be clear that, in my personal narrative on the patient records portal, I have no reason to believe that my health data had been misused by the healthcare provider or the platform provider. But patients have no visibility into what is allowed, and private entities could conceivably change their policies without notification to the consumer.

It is highly likely that if they had been in existence when HIPAA was passed, healthcare portal platforms of all kinds would have been included in the covered entity definition. Therefore, to improve the ethical collection, sharing, use, and retention of sensitive health data, it would not be inappropriate to introduce legislation to close this loophole in HIPAA and amend the law to

---

[26] *"Mental Health Apps Aren't All As Private As You Think."* Thomas Germain, Consumer Reports, 2 March 2021. https://www.consumerreports.org/health-privacy/mental-health-apps-and-user-privacy-a7415198244/.

include as covered entities electronic record-keeping and telemedicine applications that collect and hold data that would be considered PHI if otherwise held by a HIPAA covered entity.

In other words, if it's HIPAA-protected data when your doctor holds it, then it should be HIPAA-protected data when the platform holds it. Of course, this would not apply to sharing anonymized and aggregated data under government oversight for the public good as was provided for under the Affordable Care Act. Still, data ethics in a democratic society should place formal legal parameters around what private companies can do with the sensitive personal information they collect, and provide greater transparency to patients whose data is being collected.

Accountability

Up until the 2008-2010 timeframe, the Chief Data Officer (CDO) was not really a typical position in most organizations, public or private. The first CDO of a large organization in the United States is widely thought to be Cathy Doss at CapitalOne in 2002 as a response to the passage of the Sarbanes-Oxley legislation. Therefore, the impetus for the first CDO appointment was strictly focused on legal compliance. Many private sector CDOs that came after Doss were focused, and still are, on the monetization of the company's data. That is, making money off the sale of and/or generating a competitive edge using data collected on customers and partners.

With the initial focus on the bottom line, it's not surprising that public sector organizations lagged a bit, with Colorado being the first state in the United States to appoint a CDO. As of March 2022, 31 states had CDOs.[27]

The first federal-level CDO (depending on how you define the role and title) appears to have been Micheline Casey at the Federal Reserve in 2013. Federal level CDOs exploded after 2018 with the passage of the Foundations for Evidence-based Policymaking Act, which required that all federal agencies name a CDO. In parallel, the Federal Data Strategy made the establishment of a Federal Data Governance Council a priority in its Year One Action Plan.[28] As of March 2022, there were 83 CDO members of the Federal CDO Council.[29]

Why the history lesson on the establishment of the CDO?

---

[27] *"The Chief Data Officer is Here to Stay."* Colin Wood, State Scoop, 7 March 2022. https://statescoop.com/state-chief-data-officer-2022/.

[28] https://strategy.data.gov/2020/action-plan/.

[29] https://www.cdo.gov/council-members/.

*Because greater progress toward data transparency and
privacy requires accountability.*

Indeed, the Data Management Body of Knowledge (DMBoK), written and maintained by the Data Management Association-International and widely viewed as the "bible" of the discipline, notes that accountable controllers for the handling of personal information, as well as training on and oversight of ethical data practices are required for an "ethical ecosystem."[30]

The best way to achieve this accountability is to create and empower CDOs at all levels of government, as well as at non-governmental organizations and private companies that create, acquire, handle, and use data assets on a fairly large scale. What is meant by "fairly large?" Unfortunately, I can't offer a specific cut-off in terms of volume of data. Still, suppose you create derived data products for internal or external recipients that require a business intelligence tool, data catalog tool, or data processing pipeline. In that case, you probably need a Chief Data Officer.

---

[30] Data Management Body of Knowledge (DMBoK), v.2, pp 53 and 60.

Action Item

— Better Legislation —

Does your state have a Chief Data Officer position whose existence and responsibilities are codified in state law? As a citizen advocate for ethical data practices, you should find out. If the answer is no, write your state lawmakers to support legislation that creates a state-wide Chief Data Officer separate from the Chief Information Officer function. For large municipalities, a separate Chief Data Officer position is often warranted.

In many instances, it will be the leadership of CDOs at all levels of government and in non-governmental organizations with a significant impact on data collection and use that provide the initiative and direction for changes toward more ethical data practices…or away from them. While data stewards are key to any data governance program, in the absence of a CDO, identifiable data stewards who can be accountable for specific types of organizational data are absolutely essential. These accountable data roles—separate from articulated information technology roles—allow data to be seen as an asset in and of itself, rather than the byproduct of an IT tool or platform. And that separation is required for data ethics to exist in any kind of rigorous manner.

How do CDOs advance an ethical data framework in an organization? The answer is both cultural and tactical in nature. First, from a cultural perspective, it is difficult to define data ethics in an organization if data is not acknowledged as a strategic asset and made a priority at the C-Suite level. A Wharton School of Business study in 2010 revealed that a lack of awareness of one's environment and place in that environment exacerbated both the frequency and degree of ethical misconduct. People could rationalize their behavior to a greater extent when they had less context about where they and their actions fit into the big picture.[31]

The empowerment of CDOs, then, to articulate an organization's data strategy and where the collection, sharing, use, and retention of data fits into the organization's business or mission goals is a required first step in data ethics accountability. As we shall see in subsequent chapters, the leadership of an organizational CDO is what establishes the environment in which ethical data behavior can be defined and flourish. And the lack of such leadership and accountability leads to ethical missteps, intentional or unintentional.

In addition to the need for an accountable party, our democratic society also has a legal framework to ensure government accountability to the governed. These are

---

[31] Ruedy, N. E., & Schweitzer, M. (2010). *In the Moment: The Effect of Mindfulness on Ethical Decision Making.* Journal of Business Ethics, 95 (1), 73-87. http://dx.doi.org/10.1007/s10551-011-0796-y.

official records acts, such as the Federal Records Act at the national level. State-level governments have versions of official records laws that apply to state records and often to municipal records, as well. Like the freedom of information laws discussed earlier, these records laws also highlight areas that impact data ethics in a democratic society that have little to do with protecting PII. While we can argue that preserving official records is a legal issue rather than an ethical one, implementing records requirements sometimes strays out of the strictly legal realm into what could be considered an ethical dilemma.

We could look at many cases on this topic, but let's choose two: one very high profile and another that has been reported but has not received the same level of scrutiny. First, the Hilary Clinton email case. Unless one has not read or listened to the news over the past six years, they are at least somewhat aware of this case. Leaving aside the most strident of political commentary, let's examine the data ethics issue associated with records preservation. The Federal Records Act requires agencies to hold official communications and prohibits them from destroying official records. The law was amended in late 2014 to require that personal emails be transferred to government servers within 20 days, and the National Archives amended its general records schedule associated with Capstone officials, who are decision-makers at or near the top of the organizational hierarchy whose communications are subject to a higher level of preservation. But both actions were taken after Clinton left the Department of State. At the height of the brouhaha in 2015, John Wonderlich of The Sunshine Foundation told National Public Radio (NPR) that, while Clinton may not have violated the letter of the Federal Records Act as it was then written, she certainly violated the spirit of it. And there were ethical issues, in addition to potential legal ones. He told NPR, "The final arbiter of what's public or what's turned over to Congress shouldn't be private staff working for Hilary Clinton. It should be State Department employees who are bound by duty to the public interest."[32] The case never went to court, but it arguably cost Hilary Clinton the presidency.

Another, more recent and relatively less well-known case is the 2022 order from courts in Wisconsin that an investigator hired by members of the Wisconsin legislature to research election irregularities in the 2020 election stop deleting records associated with the case. As reported in the Milwaukee Journal Sentinel, in April and May of 2022, two separate judges ordered Michael Gableman, an investigator hired by the Wisconsin legislature, to cease

---

[32] Domenico Montanaro, April 2, 2015; *Fact Check: Hilary Clinton, Those Emails, and the Law*. https://www.npr.org/sections/itsallpolitics/2015/04/02/396823014/fact-check-hillary-clinton-those-emails-and-the-law.

destroying public records as he completed a taxpayer-funded review of the 2020 election.

Action Item

— Better Ethical Framework —

Ethics statements and training typically focus on data collection and use, and mention in passing (if at all) archival and preservation of data. This is an oversight regarding data ethics in public sector entities. If you are a government employee or contractor, review your agency's or department's ethics code and ethics training. If these do not include explicit coverage of the ethical responsibility to preserve records in a manner that makes them easily accessible to the public and the role such preservation plays in supporting a democratic society, advocate with the appropriate manager that materials be updated to include this content.

The judges noted that, as a former Wisconsin Supreme Court justice, Gableman should know what the records law requires and had an ethical obligation to follow it. Gableman contended he was exempt from retaining records because the lawmakers who hired him were not required to hold onto records under state law. The courts had already found Assembly Speaker Robin Vos in contempt of court for failing to release records about the election review. An attorney for the Assembly basically punted, noting that Gableman was a contractor and that the Assembly had no control over what its contractors do.[33]

However, a review of the Wisconsin Public Records Law Compliance Guide explicitly notes that the state assembly or senate is subject to the requirements of the law and that a record "also includes contractors' records. Each authority must make available for inspection and copying any record produced or collected under a contract entered into by the authority with a person other than an authority to the same extent as if the record were maintained by the authority." In June 2022, Gableman was held in contempt of court.[34]

What ethical lessons can we learn from the Clinton email and Wisconsin election records incidents? In a democratic society, there is a certain level of accountability that the government owes the governed, which mandates preserving information about government operations. The

[33] *"I'm Frankly Amazed- Another Judge Orders Republicans to Prevent the Destruction of Records in Gableman Election Review."* Patrick Markey, Milwaukee Journal Sentinel, 4 May 2022. https://www.jsonline.com/story/news/politics/2022/05/04/judge-orders-wisconsin-republicans-retain-records-2020-review/9644448002/.

[34] *"Gableman's Office Held in Contempt in Open Records case About 2020 Election Probe."* Madeline Fox, Wisconsin Public Radio, 10 June 2022. https://www.wpr.org/gablemans-office-held-contempt-open-records-case-about-2020-election-probe.

dual requirements of the Federal Records Act and the Freedom of Information Act at the federal level, and similar laws at the state and local levels, make the achievement of this accountability possible.

Here is the ethical obligation: these are laws that hope to achieve aspirational democratic goals, so it is <u>never</u> enough to adhere only to the letter of the law. Suppose a government organization is not making a concerted effort to discern and promote the spirit of these laws. In that case, there is a potential lapse in ethical public sector data practices. Such an ethical approach does not happen by accident. It must be incorporated into the onboarding and training of public sector employees and reinforced in policy and practice.

What are the ethical questions?

To leverage data "in order to form a more perfect union," data practitioners should ask themselves the following questions as they undertake data collection efforts, share and use data, and determine how long to retain data:

- Are data sources and analytical methodologies transparent to both subjects of data collection and those making decisions based on the data?

- If you are a government entity, are your transparency policies and practices inclined toward greater and not lesser transparency? (Note: if your first inclination when receiving a freedom of information request is to try to justify redacting or denying as much as possible, if your default answer to freedom of information requests is "no," then your data culture is not one of transparency, and you have some work to do to change it.)

- Are your data transparency policies and practices in line with the spirit of law and regulation, as well as the letter of it?

- If you collect personally identifiable data, are you only using it for the purpose for which it was collected? If not, do data subjects have the right to opt out of onward sharing and use of their data, or do the terms and conditions of service make it difficult or impossible for them to do so? (Note: If the terms and conditions give the illusion of choice while ensuring that most users cannot exercise that choice, then this is a data ethics problem.)

- Is there a senior-level accountable party in your organization for ethical data collection, sharing, use, and retention? Is that position adequately resourced to carry out its accountability function?

- Suppose you are a public sector employee or contractor. Are you and your supervisors adhering to both the spirit and the letter of freedom of information and official records laws and regulations? If you are aware that these laws are not being followed, have you reported your concerns either through your management chain or to your Inspector General? (Note: Being aware of such missteps and NOT reporting them is an unethical data practice.)

CHAPTER 3

Establish Justice

In matters of truth and justice there is no difference between large and small problems, for issues concerning the treatment of people are all the same.

Albert Einstein

Justice is supposed to be blind, so the use of data to inform government decisions in a just manner is squarely within the purview of data ethics in a democratic society. Too often, however, decision-makers (whether government officials at some level, private entities supporting government entities, or private entities operating in a democratic environment) fall short of this goal. This is not usually with malicious intent but rather from a lack of consideration of how data collected, shared, used, and retained impacts the creation and maintenance of a just society.

This chapter will look specifically at law enforcement and the courts as the environment for data ethics actions and decisions. Through several different case studies in which the collection or use of data has been questioned, we will discern issues to consider when entities with as much influence and power as is wielded by law enforcement and the courts leap into the process of "data-driven decision-making."

This does not mean that such organizations should avoid leveraging data to drive better decisions and actions—to the contrary. Just that they must be held to a particularly high standard since the ramifications of ethical missteps are not an unhappy customer or lost baggage—the decisions influenced by data collection and use in this arena can literally deprive people of their freedom.

Data collection

First, let's look at data collection. There is quite a bit of data collected by law enforcement organizations in the United States and collated by the FBI through the Uniform Crime Reporting (UCR) program and available through the Crime Data Explorer web-based application. This is no mean feat, given that there are roughly 18,000 law enforcement entities in the United States, and most are locally (very locally) governed.[35]

Despite a ton of effort on data collection, it is still the case that data quality is questionable, analytical results are often unreliable, and transparency leaves much to be desired. The FBI has taken steps in recent years to improve the quality of the data it collects from federal, state, and local law enforcement entities by transitioning from the Summary Reporting System (SRS) to the National Incident Based Reporting System (NIBRS).

Until very recently, the SRS mechanism established in 1930 had been the default information collection system, and the FBI acknowledged that, even with updates to allow for electronic submission and collation, the SRS mechanism was woefully outdated, lacked precision, and was of limited utility for public policymaking.[36]

The more modern NIBRS reporting process collects more complete data with greater granularity. It officially replaced SRS as the data collection standard on 1 January 2021. This does not mean that all 18,000-plus law

---

[35] Discover Policing, https://www.discoverpolicing.org/explore-the-field/types-of-law-enforcement-agencies/.

[36] https://www.fbi.gov/services/cjis/cjis-link/srs-to-nibrs-the-path-to-better-ucr-data, 2017.

enforcement entities submit data to NIBRS—reporting to the UCR is voluntary. It is, however, a step in the right direction, and the FBI provides requirements, guidelines, and federal standards to state and local law enforcement, including conducting audits regularly to ensure compliance.[37] An additional step to ensure ethical data collection and handling would be a rigorous review and update of the UCR business glossary. A request to the FBI for a copy of the business glossary for the expanded homicide reporting program yielded a fairly robust handbook. However, it was dated 1990 with a title that suggested that the information in it was current as of 1980.

Action Item

— Better Policy —

Unlike collecting data on individual private citizens, which often needs more restrictions, collecting and disseminating data on public sector entities is sometimes inadequate. Law enforcement agencies should make every effort to participate fully in both the FBI's NIBRS data collection effort and the National Use of Force database. Citizens and residents should ask their state and local law enforcement agencies if they participate in these efforts. If not, contact your state and local representatives to advocate for greater participation.

---

[37] Response from Fairfax County Police Department on their participation in the UCR program, 4 May 2022.

There is also the question of law enforcement data collection on themselves. Both SRS and NIBRS collect information on crimes that law enforcement investigated on outside individuals or groups. Law enforcement's use of force statistics is the subject of another data collection effort started in 2015: The National Use of Force collection effort. Also run by the FBI and also voluntary, the FBI reported that, in 2019, fewer than a third of law enforcement entities contributed to the National Use of Force data collection effort, representing around 40% of active-duty officers. This is a fairly new collection effort, and the hope is that additional law enforcement entities will come on board over the next few years.[38]

From the standpoint of transparency, this is an important data ethics question. As we will discuss further in the chapter on "Provide for the Common Defense," a strong democratic society requires that law enforcement, military, and intelligence agencies be held to an exceptionally high standard in their collection and use of data on citizens and residents. This oversight is only possible when sufficient data is available to evaluate these entities' activities.

---

[38] FBI National Press Office, 27 July 2020.
https://www.fbi.gov/news/pressrel/press-releases/fbi-releases-2019-participation-data-for-the-national-use-of-force-data-collection.

It's not that law enforcement agencies are (usually) intentionally hiding their activities. But as is often the case, there is sometimes insufficient attention paid to implementing laws and policies, resulting in data gaps and inequitable policy results.

In September 2021, the Montgomery County, Maryland, Office of Legislative Oversight found that the Montgomery County Police Department did not adequately collect and record information on traffic stops over a period of 14 years, potentially violating state laws. Civil rights activists expressed concern that the data that elected officials had relied upon to make public policy was incomplete and may have concealed signs of unlawful traffic stops. At the time, the executive director of the Washington Lawyers' Committee, Jonathan Smith, was quoted as saying that police departments tended to "do a really good job at collecting information on arrests, convictions, and crimes. But information around stops, searches—the quality of that data tends not to be good."[39]

---

[39] *"Montgomery Police Did Not Adequately Record Traffic Stop Data for 14 Years."* Rebecca Tan, The Washington Post, 6 September 2021. https://www.washingtonpost.com/local/md-politics/montgomery-police-traffic-stops/2021/09/02/c8fcb9d6-0b4c-11ec-aea1-42a8138f132a_story.html.

Data use

Even more common is the desire at the working level to maximize the data collected to make law enforcement more efficient. It is a laudable goal but sometimes undertaken without careful consideration of the unintended consequences. In a June 27, 2021, editorial in The Washington Post, Jameson Spivack, an associate with the Center on Privacy and Technology at Georgetown University Law School, noted that "algorithmic and surveillance technologies pervade the criminal legal system" and that "most states...don't have rules about how law enforcement can use them." He further noted that such technologies often perpetuate bias against marginalized communities because they are "trained with data that reflects human biases, resulting in predictive policing that merely sends police to already over-policed Black, Brown, and low-income neighborhoods." Finally, Spivack noted that most of these technologies and the data upon which they are based "are developed by private companies, which use copyright protections to shield their algorithms from outside inspection."[40]

---

[40] *"Maryland's Police Reform Should Include Restrictions on Predictive Technology."* Jameson Spivack, The Washington Post, 25 June 2021. https://www.washingtonpost.com/opinions/2021/06/25/maryland-police-reform-predictive-technology-restrictions/.

When neutral analysis indicates inequitable results, and the data and methodologies used to arrive at those results are hidden from view, then an ethical problem exists surrounding data use. More than any other use of data and data analysis, leveraging such methodologies to detain and prosecute individuals should be held to the highest scrutiny with the highest degree of transparency. In the absence of both these conditions, the situation threatens the very foundation of a democratic society. Let's look at a case study: the use of pre-trial risk assessment algorithms.

Pretrial risk assessment algorithms assign defendants "risk scores" to predict the chances of recidivism and general likelihood of future criminal behavior. The use of these scores varies from jurisdiction to jurisdiction, but have been used in some cases to contribute to the setting of bail, setting sentences, and even determinations about guilt or innocence. Proponents of the tools argue that they outperform judge and prosecutor judgments by using proxy data such as socioeconomic status, family background, the crime rates in the neighborhood the person lives, employment status, and a host of other data points. Critics point to two problems with the use of such algorithms: (1) the lack of transparency (the algorithms are typically considered proprietary, so the actual data used and the weighting of different factors is not available to either defendants or decision makers), and (2) third party analysis of the risk assessment scores demonstrates a significant possibility that such algorithms are racially biased against Black defendants. As a result, says the Electronic Privacy Information Center, "two people accused of the same crime may receive sharply different bail or sentencing outcomes based on inputs that are beyond their control–but have no way of assessing or challenging the results."[41]

Independent analysis of scores have indicated that Black defendants were often predicted to be at a higher risk of recidivism than they actually were. Analysis done by ProPublica found that Black defendants who did not recidivate over a two-year period were nearly twice as likely to be misclassified as higher risk compared to their White counterparts (45 percent vs. 23 percent) White defendants were often predicted to be less risky than they were. ProPublica found that White defendants who re-offended within the next two years were mistakenly labeled low risk almost twice as often as Black re-offenders (48 percent vs. 28 percent). In addition to publishing their results, ProPublica published their actual analytical

41 "AI in Criminal Justice." Ben Winters, Electronic Privacy Information Center, 2020. https://epic.org/issues/ai/ai-in-the-criminal-justice-system/.

methodology to encourage replication of the results and third party review.[42]

Despite the questions about the efficacy and equity of such "risk scores," courts have held that the use of them does not violate due process. In State vs. Loomis, the Wisconsin Supreme Court held that a trial court's use of an algorithmic risk assessment in sentencing did not violate the defendant's due process rights even though the methodology used to produce the assessment was disclosed neither to the court nor to the defendant.[43] At Loomis' trial, the trial court used an algorithm-generated risk-assessment score as a judicial tool to help in its sentencing determination, even though both the prosecution and the defense had earlier agreed to a lesser sentence as part of a plea deal. Loomis filed a motion for post-conviction relief on the grounds that the court's reliance on the score violated his due process rights.

---

[42] "How We Analyzed the COMPAS Recidivism Algorithm." Jeff Larson, Surya Mattu, Lauren Kirchner, and Julia Angwin, ProPublica, 23 May 2016. https://www.propublica.org/article/how-we-analyzed-the-compas-recidivism-algorithm.

[43] *"Wisconsin Supreme Court Requires Warning Before Use of Algorithmic Risk Assessments in Sentencing."* Harvard Law Review, 10 March 2017. https://harvardlawreview.org/2017/03/state-v-loomis/.

Action Item

— Better Policy —

The lack of visibility into the code and data associated with the development of AI algorithms by vendors is typically based upon the argument that it is proprietary information, but when those algorithms are procured for use in the public sector, particularly in law enforcement scenarios, greater oversight is warranted. Contracts for law enforcement procurement of such technologies should include, if they do not already, a requirement that the company makes available, upon request, information on the development of the algorithm and the data used to train it to a third-party reviewer under a non-disclosure agreement to assess performance and possible bias. If you are a government contracts officer, advocate for inclusion of such clauses in contracts you administer. As a citizen advocate, you can request copies of contracts with vendors through public records requests to inform yourself and your community.

Aside from the use of potentially biased data in developing algorithms used for law enforcement and judicial purposes, the <u>direct</u> use of data in the pursuit of "establishing justice" can get complicated and sometimes yield results that don't look "justifiable." Public sector organizations seeking to "treat data as a strategic asset" (which has become a mantra in data management in both the public and private sector), often try to reuse data for other purposes. While being a good steward of taxpayer resources is an ethical issue, it is a valid data ethics question as to when and whether the reuse of data for other purposes actually serves the public good. One recent example comes from reporting on police's ability to use <u>victim</u> DNA from rape kits to tie rape victims to crimes— sometimes years later. Specifically, the San Francisco Police Department appears to have used a woman's DNA from a rape kit to tie her to a property crime years later. Although the charges were later dropped and the woman has filed a lawsuit against the San Francisco Police Department, the practice may not be isolated, raising many very interesting cultural and ethical questions.

Jennifer King, a privacy and data policy fellow at the Stanford Institute for Human-Centered Artificial Intelligence, wrote in an opinion piece in The Washington Post on the case that "Including the DNA of rape survivors in a database used for criminal identification is a violation of privacy, full stop. It doesn't matter whether the rape survivor herself later commits a crime." She suggested that such a practice would violate informed consent and the right to avoid self-incrimination and that "it is not difficult to imagine how these mountains of genetic information could be abused."[44] One problem is that many states do not differentiate between victim and perpetrator DNA

---

[44] *After a Rape Survivor's Arrest, It's Time to Rethink Genetic Databases."* Jennifer King, The Washington Post, 17 February 2022.
https://www.washingtonpost.com/opinions/2022/02/17/rape-survivor-dna-arrest-in-san-francisco/.

when populating their DNA databases, and once in the system, it is not necessarily easy for someone searching the database to know the difference between victim and perpetrator DNA. Addressing this problem is actually a fairly simple data curation task, as long as it receives the appropriate attention. Unfortunately, data curation tasks typically are not a priority in digital transformation projects.

In response to the San Francisco case, in April 2022, a California State Senator proposed a bill that would prohibit including rape kit DNA of victims in investigative DNA databases, noting that "on the national level, it is already illegal to include rape kit DNA in the national DNA index...it was shocking to learn that there is no corresponding California law to prohibit local law enforcement databases from retaining the DNA from victims."[45]

But what about other states? Only advocacy at the state level will address the use of such data for law enforcement purposes. This brings us to the cultural issue.

---

[45] *"Lawmakers Look to Ban Use of Sexual Assault Victim DNA in Unrelated Cases."* Omar Abdel Baqui, The Wall Street Journal, 29 April 2022.
https://www.wsj.com/articles/lawmakers-look-to-ban-use-of-sexual-assault-victim-dna-in-unrelated-cases-11651195210.

Action Item

— Better Policy and Legislation —

Law enforcement agencies should ensure that the metadata record for DNA collection clearly shows whether DNA is victim DNA and, if it is, stipulate that it should not be included in identifying suspects. If the agency's policy is to use such DNA in an investigatory manner, at the very least, victims should be informed of this <u>at the point of data collection</u> and be allowed to opt out. Citizens and residents of any state in the U.S. should inform themselves about laws in their states regarding the use of DNA for law enforcement purposes, particularly the collection and use of victim DNA. If the law is unclear, too broad, or lacks oversight on the use of victim DNA, write your representative and advocate for change.

It is sometimes eye-opening to gather information through the anonymous comments that people write in response to news articles and social media posts. In the case of Ms. King's op-ed piece in The Washington Post, it was stunning to note how many people responded with comments along the lines of "if you don't have anything to hide, or don't commit a crime, you shouldn't have any problem with this use of data." To be blunt, this is not how our democracy is set up to work. Such an approach violates the stated and aspirational goals of the Preamble to the Constitution and the Bill of Rights; it also works against more conceptual notions of "public good."

First, the stated goals of the Bill of Rights. The Fourth Amendment to the U.S. Constitution protects against illegal search and seizure. While the US Supreme Court held in 2013 (Maryland vs. King) that anyone arrested on suspicion of having committed a crime could have their DNA taken and subsequently run through databases for links to unrelated crimes, this ruling did not apply to victims.[46] Given the 5-4 decision in the Maryland case and the fact that victim DNA was not addressed, ethics policies associated with using victim DNA for investigatory purposes should not assume that the state's interest outweighs privacy concerns.

At the very least, ethical data collection and use should consider "informed consent." It was clear in the San Francisco case—and in the reporting on it—that victims providing DNA for rape kits were never informed that their genetic material would be included in investigatory databases and that it could be used to incriminate them in future cases. In terms of the aspirational goal of the Preamble to "establish justice," and the general democratic goal of advancing public good, even if victims had been informed of this potential investigatory use of genetic data, there exists an ethical issue. Sexual crimes are already underreported, according to numerous studies over decades of research. The potential that victim DNA could

---

[46] "Supreme Court Allows DNA Testing Suspects Without Probable Cause." JB Law Criminal Defense. https://www.joelbailey.com/articles/supreme-court-allows-dna-testing-suspects-without-probable-cause.

be used against someone later for any yet-to-be-determined crime (even actions that might not today be criminal but might be criminalized in the future), would likely decrease the reporting of sexual assault even more.

Couple the use of victim DNA with the current reality that data brokers can already track and sell (to even private individuals) information from geolocation collection, and the implications for the authoritarian use of data are staggering. For example, an investigative journalist purchased a week's worth of geolocation information related to visits to Planned Parenthood clinics, showing "where groups of people visiting the locations came from, how long they stayed there, and where they went afterwards." The cost? $160.[47]

The result of such hoarding of data without probable cause, and without even rudimentary restrictions on retention and use, neither establishes justice nor advances the public good as those concepts have been typically defined in our democratic society. Some will argue that

---

[47] *"Data Broker Is Selling Location Data Of People Who Visit Abortion Clinics."* Joseph Cox, Vice, 3 May 2022. https://www.vice.com/en/article/m7vzjb/location-data-abortion-clinics-safegraph-planned-parenthood. After being "outed" by the investigative report in Vice, the company identified, SafeGraph, immediately went public saying that they were ceasing the sale of the specific Planned Parenthood datasets. This demonstrates the potential power of transparency in ensuring that private companies in the data business adhere to evolving ethical and societal norms.

collecting such vast amounts of data may one day yield the perpetrator of a heinous murder or child trafficking ring — this is, of course, true. But I argue that such individual hypotheticals are no basis for an overarching ethical framework in a democratic society, at least not without strict usage parameters, audit trails, oversight, and transparency — none of which exist with any consistency across law enforcement jurisdictions.

In addition to the data ethics issues surrounding data collection and sharing, we should also consider the justice implications of digital transformation policies that focus exclusively on the technology and give short shrift to the data collected, shared, and stored using that technology.

Let's look at the problems that have surfaced with the deployment of the Odyssey Enterprise Justice application over the past several years. The Odyssey application is a product of Tyler Technologies, a digital transformation technology provider primarily for state and local governments. Tyler is a Texas-based company with over a billion dollars in annual revenue. Its Odyssey platform, according to the publicly available brochure on its website "connects courts, prosecutors, public defenders, and the filing community through software designed to save time, eliminate redundancies, and minimize errors, so you can be more responsive to the public and share data with agencies within the justice sector."[48]

State and local jurisdictions relying on paper-based systems and/or highly manual legacy systems are certainly in need of a better way of doing things, and the Odyssey platform has been deployed in some jurisdictions with positive results. But the stories are not uniformly positive, and the pattern revealed by issues with the Odyssey platform in multiple jurisdictions is cause for concern from a data ethics perspective.

In 2016, Alameda County, California, deployed the Odyssey system. Within a few months of deployment, the public defender's office filed a motion for the county court to immediately solve the problems caused by the court's software system, Odyssey Case Manager, or abandon the technology. Twenty-six incidents were documented in the motion, although Public Defender Brendon Woods said this was "just the tip of the iceberg" regarding the number of people affected. Affected how? To start, clerks needed 20-30 minutes to input data into a defendant's file, when the legacy system required only 2-3 minutes. The backup in updating court files was significant and immediate, leading to people who had shown up for court dates being

---

[48] https://www.tylertech.com/resources/blog-articles/Brochure-Odyssey-Overview.

arrested on bench warrants because the system didn't show them as having appeared. People due to be released from jail were held days past their release dates, also because of system backups.[49]

Also, in 2016, Shelby County, Tennessee, deployed the Odyssey system with the same types of problems. In 2021, Shelby County and Tyler Technologies settled a class action lawsuit claiming that the defendants were wrongfully jailed because of errors in the Odyssey system. In 2019, the Wichita Falls, Texas, and Lubbock, Texas, deployment of the Odyssey system also led to wrongful jail issues, which the county addressed by manually checking jail rosters and instituting software workarounds. In 2022, confidential records of the State Bar Association of California were exposed because of a security flaw in the Odyssey platform. Records that were exposed included inactive enrollments due to mental illness, names of witnesses, and complainants, including juvenile records.

Is the fault in these cases, which didn't just result in an unhappy customer but violated people's fundamental civil rights, lie with the vendor or the government entity? In the

---

[49] *"Court Officials Blame Software for Wrongful Arrests, Other Legal Mishaps."* Karen Turner, The Washington Post, 20 December 2016.
https://www.washingtonpost.com/news/the-switch/wp/2016/12/20/court-officials-blame-software-for-wrongful-arrests-other-legal-mishaps/.

Shelby County case, the answer was apparently both, with Shelby County and Tyler each paying a portion of the settlement. But assigning blame does not address the underlying ethical issues. Instead, the issue may well be a distinctly cultural one. In the roll out of new applications, the primary (if not exclusive) focus is placed on application functionality and code testing. Data testing and migration are treated as secondary issues, as are critical support tasks such as training for those responsible for data entry.

Ethical data practices require that the impact on data assets be a key consideration in digital transformation initiatives, that the data risk mitigation be included in the earliest planning stages of such initiatives, that data stewards and data users have a voice in the planning and implementation process, and that rigorous training for data personnel be included in the roll out (and that such training be substantially more than a user manual hung on a Sharepoint site). If rigorous testing and training had happened in Alameda County <u>before</u> the system went live, it would not have been a surprise that the time needed for the data entry process increased by an order of magnitude. As a result, the risk to operations of the court system could have been identified and addressed before full deployment.

Government contracts, however, like many tasks in many contexts, often suffer from inertia. That is, how the last contract was written becomes how the next contract is written. Drafting new contract language and getting it through legal coordination from both the contracting party and the vendor takes time and effort. As a result, using already approved language is often seen as preferable. But this means that reasonable questions sometimes don't get asked, and when questions aren't asked, ethical missteps can occur.

For example, if rigorous training on the application for data entry personnel is not included in a contract for the procurement of digital transformation technology, it should be. If the legacy system and the data it holds are critical to the organization's mission, a pilot deployment with a full written assessment of areas of concern, before organization-wide deployment, should be strongly considered. A roadmap for data migration should be required, in addition to the roadmap for application deployment. Lack of attention to data issues in procuring and deploying mission-critical technologies constitutes a data ethics issue.

What are the ethical questions?

If you are in a law enforcement or a courts-related agency, or a citizen or resident who wants to advocate for the most ethical collection, sharing, use, and retention of data in law

enforcement and courts, here are some data ethics
questions you should ask:

- If you work for a justice-related organization, is
  data being collected and shared that highlights the
  activities of <u>both</u> the external operations and the
  internal activities of your organization? If not, why
  not? Hint: The distrust of the public and the fear
  that the public will use data to damage the
  organization's reputation is insufficient to deny
  data collection and sharing. In a democratic society,
  it is the job of justice-related entities to gain the
  trust of the public…not the other way around.

- Is data collected for law enforcement purposes
  sufficiently categorized so that victim and
  perpetrator data can be easily differentiated for
  research purposes?

- If third-party vendors are contracted to provide
  data collection and/or data analysis services, does
  the public sector agency have insight into how the
  data is collected, the specific methodologies
  employed, and any risk mitigation conducted to
  identify bias? Does the general public have insight
  into these questions? (If the answer to either
  question is "no," then you have a potential data
  ethics problem.)

- Are law enforcement officers and officers of the court sufficiently trained on the collection and use of data and derived data products that they would be able to determine whether an outlier exists that would require further investigation and follow-up? Unfortunately, training on such collection and analytical applications often is focused only on the "buttonology" of the interface, not on how to evaluate the results critically. This is not sufficient from an ethics standpoint when such results are being used to deprive people of their freedom.

- Do state records retention schedules and policies distinguish between the retention of victim data and perpetrator data?

- If you are a government contracting officer or technical representative, do contracts for technology procurement adequately address data issues and technology issues? If not, have you brought this to the attention of decision-makers in your organization and advocated for changes and updates to contract language?

CHAPTER 4

Ensure Domestic Tranquility

It is in seeing ourselves whole that we can begin to see ways of working out our differences, of understanding our similarities and of finally forming the cohesive nation that can one day experience the 'domestic tranquility' so hoped for by the framers of the Constitution.

Robert C. Maynard
American journalist and newspaper publisher

The focus on domestic tranquility in the Preamble refers to an avoidance of social strife within the new country's borders. At the time of the drafting of the Constitution, this almost certainly was specifically applied to strife between the sovereign states under the new governing structure, not intended to promote peace between individuals within those states. However, as mentioned earlier, the Fourteenth Amendment has historically been interpreted as expanding the federal government's powers to act directly to protect individual rights, superseding state actions to the contrary.

Consistent legal and regulatory requirements

In relating data ethics to the goal of ensuring domestic tranquility, we will focus on how government entities can "ensure domestic tranquility" by establishing and enforcing consistent legal and regulatory requirements. These requirements then promote standing behavioral norms around the collection, sharing, use, and retention of data that impacts individual rights and the choices that individuals have in employing technology while limiting the indiscriminate collection of personal data. Unfortunately, today's wild wild west environment is anything but tranquil.

Currently, there is clearly a legal and regulatory gap on data collection, sharing, use, and retention, which must be closed through legislation (ideally), regulatory enforcement authority, or even judicial decision.

Data industry representatives lean toward "self-regulation" or "self-policing" in opposition to legal or regulatory requirements. In concept, "self-regulation" would not be a problem, except that this is invariably code for "business (and profit) as usual," with no real regard for a consistent and rigorous ethical foundation. Indeed, the Consumer Data Industry Association does not appear even to have a formal ethical code or standard for its members.

There is not one posted on its website, and a direct request to the association to provide one went unanswered.

The problem with allowing the free market for data to act as the framework for normed behavior is twofold.

First, and more straightforward, is that there is a significant disincentive for a private company to take any action that places restrictions on its ability to profit from a commodity (and data is, in fact, a valuable commodity) in the absence of a regulatory requirement that applies to its competitors. They may WANT to act in a more ethical manner. Still, if none of their competitors are doing so, and they get no competitive advantage, it is difficult, if not impossible, to justify in a free market environment.

Second, and specifically relevant to the big data environment, is that the volume and complexity of data transactions, and the lack of transparency that consumers have into those transactions, make it difficult for people to act in their own self-interest (a stated characteristic of the Adam Smith-defined free market structure). In an environment where actions and motives are murky (at best), and the game rules vary from encounter to encounter, people cannot choose what is in their interest. And this de facto lack of freedom of choice stands in the way of our "domestic tranquility."

So, what to do?

Need for parameters

This situation argues for well-reasoned and articulated parameters around the collection, sharing, use, and retention of data—particularly personally identifiable data—by private entities in a democratic society. Efforts to pass data privacy legislation at the national level in the United States have not progressed significantly over the past several years, although there are indications that this situation may be changing. Some states have or are considering passing their own data privacy laws, in the absence of a coordinated solution at the federal level.

In the European Union, the General Data Protection Regulation (GDPR) famously gave ownership of personal data to the individual to whom the data referred. The California Consumer Protection Act (CCPA), the first significant privacy legislation in the U.S. in the big data era, was somewhat modeled on GDPR.

The Commonwealth of Virginia passed, and the Governor signed, the Virginia Consumer Data Protection Act (VCDPA) in March of 2021, but it does not come into force until January 2023. And, while the new law does give consumers a right of action and ability to access and request deletion of their data, the VCDPA appears to have some loopholes that data brokering entities can exploit. For one thing, it only applies to entities that either (1) control or process the personal data of 100,000 or more consumers during a year, or (2) control or process the personal data of 25,000 or more consumers and derive revenue or receive a discount on the price of goods or services from the sale of personal data.

The Governor of Colorado signed a data protection law in July 2021, also coming into force in 2023, with restrictions similar to the VCDPA. The Governor of Utah signed the Utah Consumer Privacy Act in March 2022, with an in-force date of December 2023. Like the Colorado bill, the threshold for companies to which the law applies is 100,000/25,000 consumers and annual revenues of more than $25 million. A law in Illinois specifically applies to biometric data has been the source of lawsuits against companies using facial scans for various purposes. Google has recently settled a class action lawsuit on alleged violations of the Illinois Biometric Information Privacy Act (BIPA) to the tune of $100 million. The ACLU won a lawsuit against Clearview AI based on the BIPA that prevents the company from selling the biometric data it collected to private entities—but does not restrict its providing the data to government entities.

These are all well and good, but they are piecemeal approaches to a national (even worldwide) issue. The piecemeal approach also has the potential negative impact of creating a patchwork of regulatory regimes in which consumers' privacy rights against a large corporate entity collecting and selling their personal information depends entirely on which side of a state border they live. In the short term, and in the absence of a national-level data privacy law, actions from Executive Branch regulatory agencies are likely to have a greater impact in creating a more tranquil data environment. One example is the recent "shot across the bow" that the Federal Trade Commission fired regarding appropriate data collection and use.

Action Item

— Better Legislation —

A bipartisan draft bill on data privacy, the American Data Privacy and Protection Act (ADPPA), was released by the House Energy and Commerce Committee in June of 2022. It provides requirements consistent across the U.S. on the collection, sharing, use, and retention of personal data by private entities; supplements existing legislation on children's privacy concerns; and establishes a Youth Privacy and Marketing Division at the FTC. While there are concerns about the preemptive nature of ADPPA and there are parts of the ADPPA that could be stronger, including a more robust private right of action, it is at least a step in the right direction. If you agree, write your congressional representatives and advocate for passage of a version of the ADPPA.

At a data privacy conference in April 2022, Federal Trade Commission (FTC) Chair Lina Khan told listeners that the existing "notice and consent" framework that applies to consumer data collection is both outdated and insufficient and that the FTC had the ability and the responsibility to assess and enforce rules around what data companies can collect about consumers and how they secure that data. For those unaware, "notice and consent" is the regulatory framework the FTC oversees that requires companies to tell consumers when they are collecting information and ask them to consent. But the notice and consent framework in its current format is roughly 40 years old and was never intended to cover the scope of activities to which it is now applied. In particular, Khan seemed to question the concept of "choice" as it applied to consumers' ability to provide consent, saying, "When faced with technologies that are increasingly critical for navigating modern life, users often lack a real set of alternatives and cannot reasonably forego using these tools." Khan acknowledged the importance of federal legislation to codify data collection requirements, but she also said that the FTC could handle enforcement within the authority given by Congress.[50]

"Optional" services

As a data ethics question, should companies be allowed to make access to critical technologies conditional on users

---

[50] "FTC Chair Pushes Privacy Rules, Calls for Limits on Data Collection." Marguerite Reardon, CNET, 11 April 2022. https://www-cnet-com.cdn.ampproject.org/c/s/www.cnet.com/google-amp/news/ftc-chair-pushes-privacy-rules-calls-for-limits-on-data-collection/.

having to agree to indiscriminate data collection and complete lack of control over what is done with that data afterward?

There are those who will argue that the providers of services that are "optional" should be allowed to define the parameters for access and that, if people don't like the terms, they can go elsewhere for the service. Let's leave aside for a moment the practical matter that reading every privacy statement and terms and conditions document to every application that even the moderate user of technology employs would take over six 40-hour work weeks.[51]

Let's try another thought experiment to answer the question from an ethical standpoint. First, imagine you are a seamstress who lives in 19th-century New York or Chicago. You are required to work 16-hour days, with one bathroom break, in an unventilated warehouse. The garment factory owner notes that people voluntarily agree to these work conditions and are free to leave and work elsewhere if they do not like the conditions of employment. But every garment factory in the city has the

---

[51] Lorrie Cranor, Professor at Carnegie Mellon, quoted in *"I Tried to Read All My App Privacy Policies. It was Over a Million Words."* Geoffrey Fowler, The Washington Post, 31 May 2022. https://www.washingtonpost.com/technology/2022/05/31/abolish-privacy-policies/.

same conditions because there is neither a legal requirement nor business incentive to do otherwise. Do you, the seamstress, actually have a "choice" and are you actually providing "consent" for these conditions?

As a data ethics issue, companies that require you to agree to terms and conditions for data collection and third-party sharing, and use the fig leaf that "the consumer can go elsewhere" if they do not agree to the terms and conditions, are typically well aware that every other company has very similar terms and conditions. The consumer really doesn't have much of a choice. In much the same way that (often violent) unionization efforts, anti-trust legislation, and fair labor standards changed the conditions that the 19th-century seamstress was forced to accept, the environment for fair data collection and use is currently under what can only be termed a societal renegotiation. This is what ensuring domestic tranquility in the 21st-century means.

Let's dig deeper into this concept of "choice" in the collection and sharing of personal data that exists in concept but really does not in reality: the collection and sharing of personal data of children. In 1998, the U.S. Congress passed the Children's Online Privacy Protection Act (COPPA). COPPA covers collecting and sharing data on children under the age of 13. It applies to online services operated for commercial purposes that are either directed towards children under 13 or have actual knowledge that children under 13 are using the service. It provides that covered applications and services must post a privacy policy; make "reasonable efforts" to notify parents regarding collection, sharing, and use of personal data; obtain verifiable parental consent; retain personal information collected only as long as is necessary to fulfill the purpose for which it was collected; and refrain from conditioning a child's participation on the child providing more information than is reasonably necessary to participate in that activity. Enforcement jurisdiction lies with the FTC.

While COPPA sounds fairly comprehensive, recent investigative reporting has found that it is all but ignored in the bulk of children's online activity. Washington Post technology writer Geoffrey Fowler found that significantly more than half of the most popular apps used by children on both iPhone and Android collect and send their personal information to marketing entities for targeted ads. Data collected most often includes general location and IP address. The loophole that application developers use? That they are (1) not "directed toward children under 13," (a fig leaf used even by the makers of Candy Crush, Angry Birds, and a coloring book app that is comprised of pictures of unicorns, dinosaurs, and ice cream) and (2) they do not have "direct knowledge" of the use of their apps by children under 13 (even though many of them simply don't ask).[52]

The problem is not just for games and other fun apps. Apps designed for educational purposes also engage in data collection and sharing. In May 2022, the FTC issued a press release warning that they "will be closely monitoring this market to ensure that parents are not being forced to surrender to surveillance" for their children to be able to use educational technology applications. We will discuss educational applications in detail in the chapter on "promoting the general welfare." For now, let's just stipulate that the ramifications could be significant if the FTC actually gets tough on enforcement: violations of COPPA carry fines of up to roughly $40,000 *per violation, per child*. In September 2019, YouTube paid an estimated $170 million fine for COPPA violations. For the purposes of context, a 2019 PricewaterhouseCoopers report estimated the global digital advertising marketing for children's data at $1.7 billion.[53]

---

[52] *"Two thirds of popular apps spy on kids"* Geoffrey Fowler, The Washington Post, 9 June 2022. https://www.washingtonpost.com/technology/2022/06/09/apps-kids-privacy/.

[53] "PwC: Kids Digital Ad Market Worth $1.7bn by 2021", Advanced Television, 12 June 2019.

What is the specific ethical concern here? It surrounds the concept of freedom of choice and the stable expectations we discussed as a precondition of "domestic tranquility."

The American Academy of Pediatrics (AAP) has researched over a period of more than ten years, the impacts of digital advertising on children. In their 2020 policy statement on the topic, the AAP noted that "school-aged children and teenagers may be able to recognize advertising but often are not able to resist it when it is embedded within trusted social networks, encouraged by celebrity influencers, or delivered next to personalized content." They further expressed "concern about the practice of tracking and using children's digital behavior to inform targeted marketing campaigns, which may contribute to health disparities among vulnerable children or populations."[54]

This policy statement indicates that the concept of "choice" when it comes to collecting and selling personal data and the resulting targeted digital advertising is all but fictitious when applied to children. The fig leaf application providers use to get around the legal COPPA requirement, that they are directed to "general audiences" and not children, is an intentional ethical misstep.

---

[54] https://publications.aap.org/pediatrics/article/146/1/e20201681/37013/Digital-Advertising-to-Children.

In many places in this book, I note that ethical missteps are more than likely unintentional and the result of a lack of understanding, training, or consideration of downstream ramifications. Not so, here: these developers and the big tech companies that host the applications are well aware that they are intentionally end-running compliance to maximize profit.

What are the ethical questions?

Ensuring domestic tranquility as a data ethics issue focuses on consistently creating and implementing policies and standards for collecting, sharing, using, and retaining personal data. This consistency contributes to the stable expectations required for society to operate smoothly. In particular, we have delved into the concept of freedom of choice and what it means for an individual to actually have a stable expectation of what "choice" is in a big data environment. Here are some ethical questions that apply to that concept:

- If you provide online services and applications, are you collecting more information than is necessary to provide the specific service? If so, why? And do users know you are collecting it and what you are doing with it? (If the answer to this last question is "yes, we disclose all of that in a 20-page terms and conditions document," then change your answer to no.)

- Do your services and applications condition access on the user providing personal data that is then packaged and sold to digital marketers? Is the sale of personal data the primary business model for the service or application, and if so, is this made clear to users (and in the case of children, to their parents)?

- If you are a public or private school, do you know if the applications and websites you recommend or require for students to complete assignments collect and sell users' personal data? If the answer is no, then ethical data practices require that you find out and act accordingly.

Chapter 5

Provide for the Common Defense

I think it's very important that the national security community, those people who do classification and declassification, take responsibility. They have to take responsibility for the handling and ultimate declassification of permanent records and particularly the secrets that they are holding in trust for the American people.

Rear Admiral Michael Studeman
Former Director of Central Intelligence
Comments for the Public Interest Declassification Board,
June 5, 2020

In the chapter on forming a more perfect union, the approach embraced was pretty strongly in favor of maximizing transparency and releasing information to the public. In this chapter, we will examine the ethics of data collection, sharing, use, and retention in an environment where full transparency is not possible.

Need for secrecy

In a democratic society, there is a necessary and healthy tension between transparency (the public's right to know about the activities of their government) and the need for secrecy in national security and law enforcement contexts. Every democratic society has provisions for such secrecy, and this secrecy does not at all imply unethical collection or use of data. There simply needs to be a recognition of the appropriate balance between secrecy and transparency, policies that ensure ethical conduct, and rigorous, independent oversight.

From an ethical standpoint, it bears noting that, in many cases, the expectations of ethical conduct for police, military, and intelligence officials go above what is expected of Joe Citizen.

Criticisms of police and intelligence conduct hold these officials to standards that would not be expected of the normal person in a democratic society. This is absolutely as it should be.

Given the powers of police, military, and intelligence officials to operate in environments of less than full transparency, with the ability of some of these entities to deprive people of their freedoms—and sometimes their lives—they <u>must</u> be held to a higher ethical standard. I realize in saying this that I may generate criticism of being anti-police or anti-military. This is not my intent at all; I stand by the assertion of "higher standard" requirements.

In terms of data ethics, the ethical standards for the collection, sharing, use, and retention of data in a secret environment should be held to particularly rigorous standards. This raises the stakes for the accountability piece of the data ethics puzzle. And it is in this vein that we will discuss what it means to have accountability when transparency is, of necessity, limited.

In 2013, The Open Society Justice Initiative published the Tshwane Principles on security and the right to information in democratic societies. The principles recognize that there is a legitimate need to withhold certain national security information, and the point of the principles was to guide those engaged in drafting, revising, or implementing laws or provisions relating to the state's authority to withhold information on national security grounds or to punish the disclosure of such information.[55]

An important part of this guidance is rigorous independent oversight of laws and policies that withhold

---

[55] https://www.justiceinitiative.org/publications/global-principles-national-security-and-freedom-information-tshwane-principles.

information and punish disclosure. Those involved in national security work often chafe at independent oversight bodies as not understanding the environment in which their mission must be accomplished. While that may be true, such independent oversight is absolutely essential to data ethics as it applies to national security restrictions on access to data in a democratic society. I say this as a former intelligence officer, myself.

It may surprise some readers that a review of the Tshwane Principles indicates that the United States actually does pretty well at adhering to this balance, despite accusations to the contrary from some watchdog organizations. U.S. law and policy meet the suggested requirements of Tshwane that:

- Private companies working in national security cannot restrict access to information on their own authority (only the government has the authority to restrict information);

- The standards for restricting access to national security information should be defined in the country's legal framework;

- Restrictions must follow the defined categories in Tshwane;

- Even national security organizations should not have a blanket exemption from disclosure laws;

- Oversight bodies should have access to otherwise restricted information; additional restrictions and requirements on the use of surveillance methods;

- Specific procedures for classifying information (including classification authorities and public access to classification rules); and

- Preservation of classified records; and time limits for the classification of information.

That said, the reason for this book is that there has been a societal shift from the collection and sharing of information in the form of narrative paragraphs to the collection and sharing of huge amounts of raw data. The intelligence discipline is not immune from the societal shift. As the collection and sharing of information has evolved, the ethical frameworks of national security agencies also need to evolve, and this need runs parallel to ongoing conversations about the overclassification of national security information in general.

Classification of information

First, before we can discuss overclassification as a possible data ethics issue, it is useful to have a primer on the national security classification authority, since many people (even some directly involved in national security work) have, at best, a rudimentary understanding of the basis of the classification system in the United States.

The classification of information (in all formats, including raw data collection) for national security purposes is done under Executive Order authority. The current Executive Order governing this activity is Executive Order 13526 (for those intelligence history nerds, 13526 was signed by then President Obama in 2009 and superseded Executive Order 12958, which itself superseded Executive Order 12356.) All federal heads of agencies with original classification authority are accountable to the requirements of Executive Order 13526, which is openly and publicly available. Implementing regulations for the Executive Order vary from agency to agency, however, so there are differences in how the requirements of the Executive Order are applied.

This is not the only restriction on access to and use of national security data. Executive Order 13556, signed in 2010 and also publicly available, governs control markings under the "Controlled Unclassified Information" program, administered by the National Archives and Records Administration (NARA). Additional controls are governed by Intelligence Community Directive 710—also publicly available—under the authority of the Office of the Director of National Intelligence. Together, classification and control markings limit access, distribution, sharing, and onward use of national security information—whether in narrative format or in digital file format. Executive Order 13526 requires anyone who has been delegated "derivative classification authority" by their respective head of agency to undergo annual training on the Executive Order requirements. The training is not centralized, but rather developed and administered by each agency, so the content varies from agency to agency.

These are the rules. Now let's turn to culture.

Culture

The Intelligence Community (IC) culture is strongly tied to the concepts of "need to know" and protecting sources and methods. While, from a policy standpoint, there has been a pendulum swing back and forth between "need to know" and "responsibility to share," the *culture* of the IC (particularly core IC agencies such as CIA, NSA, and DIA) has never *really* moved from the "need to know" concept. This is not hard to understand. The compromise of sources and methods of intelligence collection is a disastrous event for the IC, for human sources who provide information at great personal risk, and for policymakers who need to have more than just publicly available information to make the best decisions for the nation's security. That said, there is little attention paid in tradecraft training or the culture of IC agencies to the risk posed to democratic institutions of <u>too much</u> secrecy.

As a result, overclassification is a perennial problem, since almost everyone believes strongly that the risk of overclassification is minimal to non-existent, while underclassifying information carries enormous risk. This is a widely held belief, but it is wrong. Not that underclassifying carries enormous risk—it does—but that there is little to no risk in overclassification. The risk is just systemic and long-term, so harder to see on a day-to-day, case-by-case, basis. It is nonetheless a risk that can have a dire long-term impact on a democratic society. So, ethical practices in the classification of data for national security purposes is a topic that requires attention. Where should that attention come from? Better laws? Better policies?

In 2010, then-President Obama signed the Reducing Overclassification Act. The legislation was the result of the findings from the 9/11 Commission, which found that the failure to detect and act against the 9/11 hijackers was partially the result of a lack of intelligence sharing, exacerbated by both overclassification and a strong reliance on "need to know" information silos.[56] The strength of the firewall between intelligence and law

---

[56] https://obamawhitehouse.archives.gov/blog/2010/10/07/president-signs-hr-553-reducing-over-classification-act.

enforcement was a big part of the problem, but that is a topic for another day.

However, the Reducing Overclassification Act applied almost exclusively to the Department of Homeland Security, and anyone who has worked in the IC for more than 15 minutes knows that the "core" intelligence agencies don't consider the Department of Homeland Security an authority on their own intelligence collection and classification decisions. Those originating agencies retain the authority to downgrade and declassify their material.

Couple that with the fact that the Reducing Overclassification Act only applied to "homeland security" information (which is typically interpreted as specific threats against the Homeland), not information collected on a wide array of other intelligence targets. So, the Reducing Overclassification Act had little practical effect on the tendency to overclassify national security information. (Indeed, despite the fact that I spent a good chunk of my career making decisions and recommendations on classifications and controls for a core IC agency, until I started researching this book, I had never heard of the Reducing Overclassification Act.)

It is still the case that overclassifying information is a problem that hamstrings our country's ability to act in our interest (a problem made all the more stark by the global pandemic), and creates a sense of distrust between government agencies and between the government and the governed—none of which is healthy for a democracy.

What is to be done?

The ability of the general public to engage in data practices in the national security arena is, as you might imagine, limited. That said, there are some avenues for the general public to inform themselves and advocate for more transparency. Under the auspices of the National Archives and Records Administration (NARA), the Public Interest Declassification Board advises the President on the declassification of national security information for public release. They meet regularly, publish their meeting minutes on the NARA website, and announce their meetings for the public to attend virtually (you can get announcements on upcoming meetings by following NARA on LinkedIn). Many policies and procedures of the IC are published for public access on the website of the Office of the Director of National Intelligence (https://www.odni.gov/).

However, actual cultural change when it comes to classification decisions will almost certainly need to be led from the inside, if it is to happen in any kind of a timely fashion. So, the rest of this chapter is directed toward a fairly narrow audience: those government officials and contractors who work in the national security arena. You know who you are.

The best practice for programmatic accountability is often understood to align with a single accountable party; this avoids finger-pointing and confusion of "swim lanes."

However, in this case, I will depart from that best practice and assert that the accountability in classification decisions for balancing the need for secrecy with the need for transparency should rest with <u>every derivative classifier</u> of national security information. There is no other way to ensure that the vast volume of national security information classified piece by piece by an army of derivative classifiers achieves this balance. That means better, more rigorous, and more consistent IC-wide training on classification and control policies and procedures, as well as downgrade and declassification policies and procedures. Taking a yearly web-based training course that the majority of students can simply skip to and pass the multiple-choice test at the end will do nothing to change the culture of overclassification and improve transparency both within the IC and between the IC and the general public.

As it currently stands, most IC agencies have classification training that specifically checks the box of annual training required by E.O. 13526. This is insufficient for the need to address the balance between secrecy and transparency in a democratic society. Updates to training on classification and controls should go beyond E.O. 13526 content to include E.O. 13556, ICD 710, and other conceptual content like a review of the Tshwane Principles.

Action Item

— Better Ethical Framework —

Annual training on classification policy is already required of anyone with derivative classification authority, but this training is generally no more than an hour long, is not necessarily consistent across agencies, and does not put a strong emphasis on the balance between protecting information and the risk to democratic institutions posed by too much secrecy. Training on classification and controls in Intelligence Community (IC) agencies should better incorporate the need to keep information at the lowest classification appropriate with the need to protect sources and methods. Focus on only the latter creates risk and ethical implications in a democratic society. More consistent training across the IC would also help create a stable application of classification and controls. If you are a manager in a national security agency, consider advocating for more holistic derivative classification training and onboarding training. If you work in a national security agency, you don't need to wait for better training, you can read the Tshwane Principles, attend Public Interest Declassification Board virtual meetings, and generally inform yourself on your own.

Training should be more than regurgitating material on a multiple-choice quiz. Training, particularly at the onboarding stage, should be conceptual and highly interactive. Scenarios should include not only failures to protect sources and methods by underclassifying, but also failures of intelligence caused by overclassification and silo-ing of national security information.

From a policy perspective, the IC badly needs to get its collective head around large data collections and how classifications and controls should be applied to raw data collections. Techniques for protection not dependent upon assigned classification level are underused. It was once a critical part of tradecraft training in intelligence to "write for source protection" so that narrative information could be conveyed in a manner that did not reveal the source— even when the product was not classified. Even if these techniques were still a primary focus of onboarding training (a debatable point), they certainly have not made the leap into a big data collection environment.

An understanding of how file formats, file properties, and file contents can jeopardize the source or method of collection if revealed—and how they might be obfuscated to protect sources and methods while still sharing data more widely—are not terribly well understood by those responsible for policies on collecting and disseminating data. In the absence of such a clear understanding of the risk to sources and methods, the overwhelming choice of practitioners is to overclassify raw data—a classification decision that then follows the intelligence into downstream products. An IC-level working group with marching orders to rationalize the classification policy guides across all IC agencies on the application of classification and controls specific to raw big data collection would be a step in the right direction.

It would also be useful to address the issue of controlling the sharing and release of otherwise unclassified information. One of the tenets of classification tradecraft is that unclassified data sets may become classified in nature when combined with other unclassified datasets. Indeed, Executive Order 13526 Section 1.7e specifically states that: "Compilations of items of information that are individually unclassified may be classified if the compiled information reveals an additional association or relationship that: (1) meets the standards for classification under this order; and (2) is not otherwise revealed in the individual items of information."[57]

In some instances, this is interpreted "on the ground" to mean that organizations and individuals should be careful in releasing even unclassified data, because it could be combined with other unclassified data to produce material that could meet the standards of national security classification policies. That would be a misinterpretation of E.O. 13526 and a slippery slope that would, logically, lead to almost anything being withheld. The E.O 13526

---

[57] https://www.archives.gov/files/isoo/notices/notice-2017-02.pdf.

subsection is meant as a derivative classification decision based on the specific <u>compiled, derived product</u>. That means the organization compiles the two unclassified datasets, and the classification determination is made at that time. It is <u>**not**</u> meant to restrict the release of otherwise unclassified information on the assumption that it could—in some theoretical instance in some theoretical future—be combined with something else by a third-party and reveal potentially classified information. Classification and control policies and training should make this clear to all derivative classifiers.

What are the ethical questions?

If you work for a national security agency, as either a government employee, industrial contractor, or independent contractor, there are specific issues that you should consider from a data ethics perspective. This is particularly true when balancing the need for secrecy with the requirements for transparency in a democratic society:

- Review your organization's classification and control implementing regulations. Is there any mention of the need to balance secrecy with the need for transparency in a democratic society, or are they fundamentally ONLY about classifying material to protect secrecy? If the latter, then these policy documents are incomplete from a data ethics standpoint.

- Does your agency's training (either onboarding or annual re-training) cover the need to balance secrecy with the need for transparency in a democratic society?

- Is your default answer for requests from other IC agencies for sharing of raw data "no?" If so, suggest to organization decision-makers that policies and procedures be reviewed to increase data sharing and increase both mission accomplishment and transparency.

- Is it the policy or practice of your organization to "err on the side of caution" in releasing unclassified data because it could possibly be combined with other unclassified information in the future to reveal a classified compilation? If so, point out to organization decision-makers and legal components that this practice may be inconsistent with both the spirit and letter of E.O. 13526.

- Have your policies, procedures, and classification guides been updated to account for data collection characteristics, in addition to more traditional information collections?

CHAPTER 6

Promote the General Welfare

> *The true basis of morality is utility; that is, the adaptation of our actions to the promotion of the general welfare and happiness; the endeavor so to rule our lives that we may serve and bless mankind.*

Annie Besan
British writer, philanthropist, women's rights activist

Let us not attempt to discern the Founding Fathers' specific intent to promote the general welfare. There is no hard and fast definition of either "general" or "welfare" in the Preamble to the U.S. Constitution. Any attempt to define these terms at the national level could change at the state and local levels. Instead, as we look at the application of data ethics to a framework based upon the Preamble, it is more useful to look at the evolution of the concept of general welfare from a societal standpoint and ask how the collection, sharing, use, and retention of data either advances or stymies that goal.

Social rights

Societal or social rights, by definition, are the result of a social contract. What does this mean in a democratic society? Like many other topics discussed in previous chapters, this can be a matter of debate.

For the purposes of this discussion, however, we will take as a working definition the one posited by the United Nations High Commissioner for Human Rights. This working definition includes the rights of people to achieve adequate food, adequate housing, education, health, social security, water, and sanitation, and to take part in cultural life, and to work.[58]

While the implementation of this definition in the United States has often focused on the fair adjudication of societal or social rights—rather than ensuring that every citizen has a specific level of healthcare or an education or a minimal standard of living—at the very least, in the ethics of data in our democratic society, we should strive for an environment in which our collection, sharing, use, and retention of data does not present a hurdle to those social rights. It can be argued, however, that data collected by government entities (or on behalf of government entities), that is not then put to use advancing social rights, risks

---

[58] https://www.ohchr.org/en/human-rights/economic-social-cultural-rights.

potential ethical problems under common good ethical standards. Let's look at two case studies—one in which efforts need to be made to ensure data collection and use does not present a hurdle to social rights, and another in which data has been put to active use in advancing social rights.

Education

The use of data to improve educational outcomes at the societal level could be interpreted as an important part of providing for the general welfare, since most of those living in a democratic society would tend to agree that a populace with at least basic education is necessary to engage in civic activities. And both government and non-profit organizations have supported the collection and use of data to promote the "public good" in the education arena.

Teri Hinds, a consultant with First San Francisco Partners who has nearly two decades of experience focusing on data management in higher education, notes that work is being done by organizations such as the Association for Institutional Research, the American Association of Collegiate Registrars and Admissions Officers, and the Data Quality Campaign to create definitions and parameters for data collection and use specifically in higher education. Hinds also says that there is an increasing focus on equity in education data collection and use, with both data users and data subjects asking questions like "who is interpreting this data?" and "who has a seat at the table when data collection and use decisions are made?" She also noted that more and more often, there are questions about access to and use of aggregated cloud-based data by third-party vendors for their own purposes, which often have nothing to do with educational goals. Much of this new data collection comes from what Hinds calls the "well-intentioned surveillance" of students.[59]

To discuss the "promotion of the general welfare," we will focus first on this idea of "well-intentioned surveillance," because, on the surface, those undertaking these actions tend to have the general welfare as their goal. Too often, though, students (even those students at colleges and universities who are legal adults and entitled to all the rights of adults) have little to no input into data collected on them and how that data is used, shared, and retained. Educational institutions are often not well-equipped to act as advocates for students with tech companies and platforms.

---

[59] Interview with Teri Hinds, First San Francisco Partners, 25 April 2022.

While it is true that, in the United States, the Family Educational Rights and Privacy Act (FERPA) provides some data collection, sharing, and use protections, there is a lot of data about students that does not rise to the level of "educational records," and which exist in a legal "grey" area. FERPA was passed in 1974, and all updates since then have been regulatory, not actual legal updates. According to Hinds, this often leaves individual schools stuck with the question, "When have we gone too far?", without much guidance on where those lines should be drawn.[60]

However, a legal grey area does not need to constitute an ethical grey area. To illustrate the point, let's look at a few recent examples. Before proceeding, let's be clear that none of the issues highlighted below are meant to suggest that vendors or schools are intentionally acting unethically. Rather that the data ethics conversation so far has been incomplete and needs to evolve (and quickly) if unethical use of student data is to be avoided in the future.

The COVID pandemic starting in 2019 (still ongoing as this is being written) upended the delivery of elementary and secondary education across the country. As schools pivoted from classroom-based to virtual learning, there were many hiccups and missteps, which was to be

---

[60] Interview with Teri Hinds, First San Francisco Partners, 25 April 2022.

expected. However, some of these hiccups had significant data privacy and ethical impacts that will long outlast the pandemic. For example, in addition to strictly educational uses, the Baltimore City school system monitored the laptops it provided to students not only for virtual learning, but also including the use of software that alerted officials when a student might be considering suicide.[61]

While some mental health professionals applauded the use of technology to identify students at risk for suicide—and there were instances of children being referred to emergency personnel for evaluation—there were, and are, substantial data ethics quandaries to address, including access to and downstream uses of the collected data. What seems to be missed is what can and should be done with the collected data once the school has it.

The GoGuardian Beacon software, the tool used by Baltimore City Schools, notes in its marketing materials that it operates "continually at the browser level," which basically means that it would sweep up everything the student does anywhere online—not just the use of educational applications. To their credit, the Beacon

---

[61] *"Baltimore School Laptops Monitored for Safety and mental health Reasons, Officials Say."* Liz Bowie, The Washington Post, 24 October 2021.
https://www.washingtonpost.com/local/education/baltimore-school-laptops-monitored/2021/10/24/be2c6b6e-2d2a-11ec-8ef6-3ca8fe943a92_story.html.

product guide notes that they "do not sell Personal Student Information…do not use Personal Student Information to target advertisements or market to students or anyone else, to amass a profile about a K-12 educational student for a non-educational purpose, or for any purposes prohibited by the Family Educational and Privacy Rights Act (20 U.S.C. § 1232g; 34 CFR Part 99.3) ("FERPA"), California Business & Professions Code section 22584 ("SOPIPA"), and California Education Code section 49073.1." GoGuardian also stipulates that "at all times, Personal Student Information is the property of and under the control of a School," that "each School determines which Authorized School Personnel have access to the School's account," and that GoGuardian "may share or disclose information, including Personal Student Information, to third parties pursuant to a School's instruction or with a School's permission."[62]

However, there are questions of analytical rigor and equity for applications that are using online activity data to flag inappropriate or dangerous behavior. It is unclear to users (students or schools) what datasets the applications like Beacon are trained on and whether those datasets are normed for cultural differences in speech patterns, word choices, or video selections. In response to a direct request

---

[62] https://www.goguardian.com/policies/product-privacy.

for information about the proxy data that their algorithm is trained on, whether they conduct any assessment for racial or cultural bias of that data, and the training that their own operators undergo in interpreting algorithmic results, GoGuardian declined to provide any information not already on its website (which does not include answers to any of the above questions).[63]

A Maryland Public Records Act request to Baltimore City Schools for contract details with GoGuardian was answered, but without any information specifically about the restrictions on data collection, sharing, use, or retention or what could be done with data by any subsequent company that might acquire GoGuardian. The Baltimore City School's answer to a specific question about contract terminology on these topics was "the standard terms of use and terms of service set forth on GoGuardian's website currently govern student use and privacy standards. Thus, this information is not currently reflected in a contract between City Schools and GoGuardian."[64] In other words, GoGuardian alone decides what GoGuardian can do with the data. And while their current terms of use seem fairly well defined, there is no legal restriction against their

---

[63] Email from GoGuardian, 20 April 2022.

[64] Maryland Public Records Response, 10 August 2022.

simply changing their mind or an acquiring company deciding to use or retain the data differently.

In addition to contractual restrictions on data practices, training is also an issue. A parallel request for Baltimore City Schools training materials for teachers on the Beacon application was limited to the "buttonology" of how to set up and use accounts; there was no content on how the results of the algorithmic analysis might be used.

On top of the concern about the collection and sharing of student data by the vendor, there is a parallel "public good" concern regarding the use of data by schools themselves. There is evidence that students are not treated equitably in this "well-intentioned surveillance" arena, and data-use "creep" for disciplinary purposes—not just mental health welfare is increasingly leveraged by school administrators. In August of 2022, a group of educational and civil liberties organizations signed and sent a letter to the Department of Education urging greater protection for particularly students of color, LGBTQ+ students, and students with disabilities when it came to the use of surveillance technologies. Research from The Center for Data and Technology cited in the letter indicated that data from these applications significantly increased student disciplinary actions, contact with law enforcement (with students of color disproportionately impacted), and instances of LGBTQ+ students being "outed" as a result of online activity.[65]

There is also an equity issue with data collection, sharing, and use based on income level since tracking applications are required only for school-owned devices. Students with the wherewithal to purchase and use personal devices often aren't subject to the same level of scrutiny—this is both an issue of equity and analytical integrity, as the datasets then become skewed to an identifiable subset of the student population. In a September 2021 report, "Online and Observed: Student Privacy Implications of School-Issued Devices and Student Monitoring Software," The Center for Democracy and Technology noted that there was evidence that students using school-issued devices are monitored to a greater extent than their peers using personal devices and that districts with wealthier student populations reported that their students are more likely to use personal devices, which are subject to less monitoring than school-issued ones.[66]

---

[65] Center for Data & Technology, 3 August 2022. https://cdt.org/insights/letter-to-ed-office-for-civil-rights-on-discriminatory-effects-of-online-monitoring-of-students/.

[66] *Report: Online and Observed.* DeVan Hankerson Madrigal, Cody Venzke, Elizabeth Laird, Hugh Grant-Chapman, and Dhanaraj Thakur , Center for Democracy and Technology, 21 September 2021. https://cdt.org/insights/report-

This becomes a more inequitable situation when the data collected from the tracking applications begin to be used for disciplinary purposes, rather than simply safety concerns. Low-income students were significantly more likely to have these negative interactions, because they only had their school-provided device for online activity. Higher income students typically use personal, unmonitored devices outside of school uses.

In addition to a lack of appropriate guardrails around surveillance technologies, there is also evidence that K-12 applications designed primarily for educational purposes gather data on students that the third-party vendor then passes to marketing companies. A 2022 study from the Human Rights Watch advocacy group covering 164 educational applications and websites determined that the vast majority of educational applications were designed to send information they collected to ad technology companies. In many cases, data collection and transfer were not specifically disclosed in privacy policies. Researchers also found that most schools conducted no technical privacy impact analysis before acquiring educational applications or endorsing websites.[67] This is

---

online-and-observed-student-privacy-implications-of-school-issued-devices-and-student-activity-monitoring-software/.

[67] *"Educational Apps Track Students' Private Data."* Drew Harwell, Washington Post, 24 May 2022.

not surprising, as most school districts do not have the resources or expertise to do much more than ask superficial questions at a demo presentation.

In such cases, the contract with the vendor has really been the only protection schools (and students) have in ensuring that data is not used for purposes for which they have not provided express consent. These contracts should be accessible to anyone under most states' freedom of information laws.

The one between the Fairfax County, Virginia, school system (one of the largest and most diverse in the country) and Schoology includes fairly strong and well-worded restrictions on access control, cybersecurity, and onward use of data. It also includes a "Covenant of Confidentiality" that limits third-party sharing to only entities that are also bound by the confidentiality agreement and limits the use and sharing of data to only that which directly supports the vendor's contractual agreement. So far, so good. The main loophole? The confidentiality requirements do not apply to directory data for which the student has not opted-out, nor for de-identified data. This is actually a pretty big loophole, since Fairfax County defines directory data as potentially

---

https://www.washingtonpost.com/technology/2022/05/24/remote-school-app-tracking-privacy/.

including student name, parent or guardian name(s), birthdate, school, grade, primary home language, and parent/guardian contact information.[68]

Students are automatically "opted-in," and a form must be completed to opt out. The form has various options for different restriction levels, which are included in a 13-page "Opt Out Booklet." This type of policy may have been sufficient in the pre-big data realm, but now that almost every school has some type of contract with a third-party Learning Management System (LMS) vendor, and enormous amounts of student data can and is collected on these platforms, making "opting out" a strenuous process should constitute a data ethics question. While I am not at all suggesting that Schoology is doing anything untoward with Fairfax County student data—or anyone else's—the fact remains that the contract <u>does</u> appear to allow the vendor (or any subsequent company who buys them out) a fairly large loophole to package and monetize such data if they chose to do so. It is in this environment that the FTC issued the May 2022 warning to educational technology companies (mentioned in a previous chapter) that they would be watching to ensure strict compliance with both the letter and spirit of COPPA requirements.

_____

[68] https://oldecreekes.fcps.edu/resources/parent-handbook/student-directory-information.

Action Item

— Better Policy —

Schools that collect student data should not rely solely on broad FERPA or COPPA legal requirements to govern data collection, sharing, use, and retention. No collection of personal data should be undertaken without a well-defined governance structure that includes, at a minimum, who is accountable for the data collection program, including approval of onward use and sharing of data; a well-articulated access control policy that includes sanctions for unauthorized access; data retention and disposition policies; and required training on data use for those accessing and using collected data. If you are a school official, parent of school-aged children, or just a concerned citizen, consider actively advocating for such language in contracts with educational platforms and strict data policies and training at the school board level.

Other examples of potential problems with the collection and use of student data exist at the post-secondary education level. The following case studies are different in one particularly notable fashion, which we will dive into in a bit: in the case of the SpotterEDU application, new data is being collected by the vendor on students; in the case of DegreeAnalytics, the vendor is analyzing existing data collected on students by the university. Why is this important? From a data governance perspective, the direct ability to ensure ethical sharing and use of data rests with a different entity and the actions taken vary.

SpotterEDU is a student tracking application used on college and university campuses that monitors attendance in class. It uses an app on the student's phone coupled with SpotterEDU iBeacons mounted in classrooms to confirm a student (or rather a student's phone) is in class. The idea is to automate attendance monitoring through BlueTooth technology so that teachers don't have to take class time to do so. Originally designed as a verification application to monitor attendance for student athletes, whose playing eligibility required verifiable class attendance, it has expanded on dozens of college campuses to include the entire student population.

While SpotterEDU's website notes that it only tracks students in class—not in other locations—that is entirely based upon where the iBeacons are located and could well be expanded to locations other than class (such as libraries, dormitories, and other campus locations). It would also be remiss not to question whether "data-driven decision-making" is an ethical goal if organizations know their data is of questionable quality. According to Washington Post reporting, SpotterEDU's own terms of use said its data was not guaranteed to be "accurate, complete, correct, adequate, useful, timely, reliable, or otherwise."[69] Because

---

[69] *"Big Brother on campus: Monitoring stirs debates."* Drew Harwell. The Washington Post, December 25, 2019.
https://www.washingtonpost.com/technology/2019/12/24/colleges-are-turning-students-phones-into-surveillance-machines-tracking-locations-hundreds-thousands/.

the SpotterEDU iBeacons collect this data, schools have limited ability to audit or correct data holdings.

Finally, reviews of the SpotterEDU app on the Apple App Store are not positive. They include such feedback as "I'm convinced Satan himself invented this app so that, instead of paying attention in class, you spend the whole time trying not to be counted absent and penalized."[70]

The tracking application that Virginia Commonwealth University (VCU) implemented as a pilot in 2019, on the other hand, was not SpotterEDU; it was Degree Analytics. Unlike SpotterEDU, which has proprietary iBeacons that collect data on student location directly, a review of the Degree Analytics contract with VCU obtained via a Freedom of Information Act request (yes, I'm aware of the irony), reveals that Degree Analytics only used access to data (including Wi-Fi logs) that VCU already collected on students, that no data left VCU systems, and that Degree Analytics reports based upon educational records covered by FERPA were themselves also covered by FERPA restrictions. The contract, frankly, laid out a fairly decent governance structure to ensure the ethical use of student data. The problem here appears to have been at least partially with communication. None of the above caveats from the contract were communicated clearly to students,

[70] https://apps.apple.com/us/app/spotteredu/id943470736.

and the notification and opt out period was less than two weeks before implementation.

When data collection, sharing, use, and retention policies are not made transparent to subjects, the organization collecting the data should not really be surprised when there is pushback. In the VCU case, the independent student newspaper, the Commonwealth Times, sowed doubts about the Degree Analytics program's secrecy and stated mission. In an opinion piece entitled "They're Watching You," the opinions editor wrote, "I can bet a large sum of students didn't know — still don't know — about the implementation of Ram Attend. I mean, how could they? The opt out form was hidden in just another email…If VCU truly wanted this program to be optional…[it] would have been announced in a more fashionable way catered to students such as an Instagram or Twitter post. We all know most students just scroll past emails from VCU. I know that if the university wanted students to be fully aware of the program, they would have introduced it in a manner much more discoverable and noticeable."[71]

---

[71] *"Tea Time With Tagwa: They're Watching You."* Tagwa Shammet, The Commonwealth Times, 19 November, 2019.
https://commonwealthtimes.org/2019/11/19/tea-time-with-tagwa-theyre-watching-you/.

The organized "opt out movement" spread quickly over social media and climbed to more than half of all eligible students (The VCU read-out on the pilot noted that—of 4047 students eligible—2421 chose to opt out). In the end, the pilot lasted only a single semester before VCU concluded that automated Wi-Fi connectivity-based attendance recording "is not the best tool for VCU at this time."[72]

A lack of clear and timely communication speaks to the "transparency" issue discussed in chapter two. Subjects of data collection need sufficient insight to make an informed decision about data collection. While there are typically opt out options in student tracking applications, these options are not often made easy to find or understand. For example, in one case, students opted out by clicking "no" on a window that asked whether they wanted to help "support student success, operations, and security."[73]

As noted by the student op-ed piece, communicating information in a channel and format that administrators are aware is typically ignored by students is also problematic. Students, therefore, are not often really aware that they can opt out or how.

---

[72] https://semss.vcu.edu/ram-attend/.

[73] " Big Brother on campus: Monitoring stirs debates." Drew Harwell, The Washington Post, December 25, 2019.

As so often is the case when the risk of ethical missteps rises, the cases detailed above—as well as numerous other student monitoring cases across the country—appear to have begun with the best intentions.

> *The data ethics issue is not in the <u>intent</u>, however; it's in the implementation, and it's in the loopholes.*

The issue arises when the people in decision-making positions stop asking the inevitable "what if" questions. In many cases, monitoring capabilities were deployed without <u>remotely</u> sufficient attention paid to ethical "guardrails," essentially governance and ethics policies associated with data collection, sharing, use, and retention.

Health

If healthcare and health outcomes were not already at the forefront of the "general welfare debate" in the United States, the global COVID pandemic certainly made sure those topics jumped to the front of the line. Early in the pandemic, contact tracing applications jetted into discussions on how to best use data to protect people's health, with parallel concerns about the collection of personal data, its use, security, and retention. But COVID contact tracing is not the case study we will look at in this discussion of data ethics and "promoting the general welfare."

For this health case study, we will look at what can only be considered a highly successful data ethics effort. One that identified a public good, gathered data in a manner that was carefully considered and balanced, and was transparent in its analysis, results, and processes. It offers "lessons learned" to other public sector organizations and private sector partners seeking to implement similar projects. The case study is the Framework for Addiction Analysis and Community Transformation (FAACT) project in the Commonwealth of Virginia.

In 2016, fatal drug overdoses became the number one cause of natural deaths in Virginia.[74] The Virginia Secretary of Health and Human Services, Dr. Bill Hazel, a strong advocate for the use of data to improve health outcomes, pushed for legislation that, in 2018, not only required the creation of the Virginia Chief Data Officer position, it specifically required that the CDO undertake a pilot data sharing program on the opioid crisis.[75]

The Health and Human Services department in Virginia had already tried on its own to increase data sharing at the

---

[74] https://www.nascio.org/.

[75] Virginia's Government Data Collection and Dissemination Practices Act.

state level through an "Expanded Memorandum of Understanding" (EMU) but had gotten little traction in adoption. Even when adopted in point-to-point transactions, the EMU lacked the infrastructure to efficiently and securely share data. This issue was the first order of business for the newly appointed Chief Data Officer of Virginia, Carlos Rivero. Rivero had little in the way of financial or personnel resources, but was able to partner with a private platform vendor, the Virginia Department of Criminal Justice, and local organizations in the Winchester, Virginia, area eager to be the pilot project's test bed, given the impact of the opioid crisis on their population.

Bringing together datasets from local organizations—including those working in healthcare, law enforcement, and social services—Rivero created a Data Trust environment that included not only the technical protection of shared data, but data governance and privacy policies and procedures that made transparent to all data providers and users the same stable expectations of data sharing and use and enabled the CDO as the accountable "trustee" of shared data assets. The project created dashboards using the same underlying data but tailored for the recipient's own mission perspective. The results exceeded expectations for a pilot project.

In January 2019, there began to be a spike in fatal opioid overdoses, from just four deaths in January to ten deaths in

February alone, and then 14 deaths in March. Using data to pinpoint the spike and the locations of overdoses, participating organizations realigned resources quickly to respond. The Virginia State Police redistributed their investigative resources to specifically track the source of drugs causing the fatal overdoses. By focusing on specific cases highlighted in the dashboard, they quickly determined that the drug in question had been laced with fentanyl. This allowed hospitals to update their treatment protocols to assume fentanyl overdose when an opioid case presented. Social services groups were able to put out Public Service Announcements to substance abuse counselors and other organizations close to the community warning of fentanyl-laced heroin in the region. In April of 2019, the Winchester, Virginia, area had zero fatal opioid overdoses.[76]

In the months that followed, the FAACT pilot program grew its Data Trust environment to include state-wide datasets, created a Data Governance Council and an Executive Data Board, deployed the Virginia Open Data Portal and Enterprise Data Catalog, made basic data governance training available to all state employees, and posted all its data governance artifact templates on its public-facing website.

---

[76] Carlos Rivero interview, 19 April 2022.

Following the successful pilot, in January 2020, then-Governor Ralph S. Northam implemented the Commonwealth of Virginia Data Trust and statewide data governance framework through Executive Order 48, just in time for it to be leveraged for the state to quickly address its data and analytics needs to appropriately respond to the COVID-19 pandemic a few months later. This paved the way for the Virginia Hospital and Healthcare Association, a private organization, to join the data trust in March 2020, providing the necessary intelligence to make data-driven decisions in the midst of the global pandemic.

In retrospect, Rivero, who left the Virginia CDO position in November 2021, said the technical implementation was easy. It was confidence building among state agencies that was hard, adding that it was the governance framework, not the technical tools, that started to build trust and change the way people interacted over the use of data for public good.[77]

Rivero also undertook a months-long CDO Roadshow, traveling state-wide to explain how the CDO as trustee of state data assets would assume accountability for ensuring shared data was protected and used properly. Finally, Rivero emphasized how the public-private partnership with their platform vendor, who provided first-rate

---

[77] Carlos Rivero interview, 19 April 2022.

technical and analytical tools but laid no claim to programmatic data (aggregated, anonymized, or otherwise), helped make the program a success.

What are the ethical questions?

Even when an identifiable public good has been articulated for the collection and use of data, there need to be parameters around that collection and use. There also should be <u>real</u> accountability, meaning those accountable have the requisite knowledge and training to act in that capacity. What ethical questions should be asked in such a case to ensure that data collection, sharing, use, and retention truly "promote the general welfare?"

- Is there documentation on what data is being collected and for what purpose, and is that documentation made available in an easy-to-understand language to the subjects of the data collection?

- Are there written policies and procedures for who has access to sensitive personal data?

- Who is accountable for approving access to data? And for withdrawing access once an individual's justifiable need for access to the data no longer exists?

- What are the retention requirements for the data, and can subjects request deletion of their data? If not, why not? (Hint—if the answer is "because the company's business model is to profit from collected data indefinitely," that is a potential data ethics pitfall.)

- Are those collecting, monitoring, and taking action on the data trained on how to handle and interpret it?

- When data collection results from a public-private partnership, is there a non-proprietary version of the agreement between the vendor and the public entity that provides the public insight into government activities without releasing company proprietary information?

- When third-party vendors collect data on behalf of government entities, is it clear who owns the data in the contract? If third-party vendors are contractually able to access and use the data for purposes other than the direct mission of the government organization, are there restrictions on this activity, and is the collection and use of data made absolutely transparent to citizens and residents?

CHAPTER 7

Secure the Blessings of Liberty

...that this nation, under God, shall have a new birth of freedom—and that government of the people, by the people, for the people, shall not perish from the earth.

Abraham Lincoln
Gettysburg Address

Some readers will likely have been rubbed the wrong way at some point during this data ethics discussion. I want to acknowledge that. I may have criticized a practice in which your organization engages and feels strongly about it being called ethically questionable. You may not agree with some of the suggestions for advocacy. I may have called out examples reported in the media of ethical missteps that strike a bit too close to home.

While acknowledging these areas of potential "push-back," I stand by my criticisms. The criticisms, however, should be taken in the context of structural, systemic criticisms (for the most part), rather than accusations lobbed at particular individual or organizational actors. Our big data environment suffers from the legacies of the digital technology "origin story," one that considers only the opportunities of new technology and minimizes attention to the costs—to both individuals and society as a whole. So, discussing "blame" for harmful or inadequate data ethics practices will only get us so far.

Realizing and articulating the structural systemic issues associated with a data ethics void is the first step to addressing it as a society. This is an absolute necessity since punishing a specific ethical violation in a vacuum will not change the data culture significantly or quickly. Make no mistake, the current data ethics environment must change. So how do we advance a data ethics environment with a better chance of "ensuring the blessings of liberty to ourselves and our posterity?"

The quotation from Abraham Lincoln's Gettysburg Address that headlines this final chapter may seem a bit gratuitous, but it actually highlights something that needs to always be remembered in the discipline of data ethics: people.

People, not automated systems, make ethical decisions. People, not abstract concepts or data points, are impacted (negatively or positively) by the collection, sharing, use, and retention of data. In a democratic society, abdicating our personal responsibility for ensuring ethical data practices means abdicating our responsibility to the democratic society itself. Although the previous chapters have been organized according to the aspirational goals of the Preamble to the U.S. Constitution, during the course of those previous chapters, I hope you have noticed several overlapping themes have emerged that form the basis for an ethical framework in a democratic society. In the paragraphs below, I have tried to organize these overlapping themes into some *dimensions of data ethics*.

It is no accident that these proposed criteria for ethical data practices resemble data quality dimensions. Dimensions of data quality can articulate the parameters of both "fitness for purpose" (i.e., the data is relevant to the analytical question) and "fitness for use" (i.e., the data has the characteristics required to provide an answer to the analytical question) in data analysis.

In a democratic society, I posit that these ethical practice criteria should be seen as something like a "wrapper" for fit for purpose and fit for use evaluations, answering the question of *"fit for intent."* Data may be both fit for purpose and fit for use, but not fit for intent.

Just because you CAN do something with data, doesn't mean you SHOULD do something with data.

I want to make clear that "fit for intent" does not, in any sense, mean that I am advocating for cherry-picking data projects to advance specific political agendas (on either side of the political aisle). That's not what I mean by intent. The definition of intent in this sense is as follows:

For a government entity, the intent should be to actively advance an identifiable and articulated public good; for a non-government entity operating in a democratic society, the intent should be to <u>not present a hurdle</u> to the public good in the pursuit of your organizational bottom line.

Here are some initial ethical data practice criteria to consider by government, non-government, and private sector entities in a democratic society.

Transparency

In a democratic society, transparency is essential to ethical data practices. This is particularly true for actual government entities that are required by law to make information about the operations of government available to citizens and residents. There are—or should be—some basic transparency requirements on the collection, sharing, use, and retention of personal data on individuals that also apply to companies and non-governmental organizations in a democratic society. We have seen that we often fall short on both scores.

When designing ethical codes and policies on data collection, sharing, use, and retention, transparency should be a key consideration. When developing training and onboarding material on data collection, sharing, use, and retention, transparency should be explicitly covered and included in learning objectives.

Accountability

Ethical practices do not happen by accident. For a true ethical culture around data practices to develop and exist in an organization or in a society, there needs to be accountability. This can mean an internal accountable party (such as a Chief Data Officer), an independent oversight body, and the entire workforce or population. In fact, true accountability in a democratic society encompasses all three. And this is where true accountability is dependent upon a certain degree of transparency. When drafting laws, regulations, and policies in a democratic society, ensure that an accountable party is identified and given sufficient authority and resources to act as such.

Analytical rigor

There are no shortcuts in producing data-driven analysis. People like to say that "the data doesn't lie." Please. Data lies all the time; or if data doesn't lie, it at least misleads, both unintentionally and (unfortunately sometimes) intentionally.

Any organization, governmental or non-governmental, that collects data for research, conducts data analysis, and/or produces data-derived products should have both an analytical code of ethics and analytical training for practitioners. That code and those training programs should include explicit identification of and learning objectives tied to the tenets of publication ethics and the identification of potential bias in data and data products.

Fairness

What is fair? This is a complicated question in ethics discussions in general, and emphatically so in the practice of data ethics. This complexity stems from the assumption that if you have data to back up your point, that point must, ipso facto, be taken as valid. After all, "data doesn't lie." As noted above...not so much.

So, part of ensuring analytical rigor is the initial consideration of the ethical dimension of fairness. For fairness to exist in a data ethics sense, data collection efforts should consider multiple perspectives. Data categorization and tagging schemes should consider possible downstream use of data and whether it is not only analytically sound to use such data for that purpose, but it is *fair* to use data for certain downstream purposes. If the downstream use of data disproportionately and negatively impacts an identifiable group, this is a red flag that bears further examination before proceeding.

Protection

Protection as a data ethics issue is twofold: the protection of personally identifiable data itself (which is a common topic often seen as a largely technical issue), and the protection of the actual human subjects of that personally identifiable data (which is often overlooked in technical program management).

The former issue of protection entails the use of aggregation and anonymization techniques, only collecting the data needed for the purpose, and making it easy for people to opt out of data collection and third-party sharing. The latter issue requires a more in-depth discussion of informed consent and the concept of choice in a big data environment. Ethical data practices need to incorporate an understanding of vulnerable populations (such as children, the elderly, and traditionally marginalized communities) and ensure that terms and conditions for application use and data collection are made available to users in an articulate fashion.

If law, regulation, and policy in a democratic society began to reflect these data ethics dimensions (in both letter and spirit), systemic and structural flaws in current practice could be largely addressed. But it will take a multi-pronged approach of all three norm-creating efforts—law, regulation, and policy—to create such a framework. This means sustained effort in advocacy, sufficiently staffing and resourcing regulatory agents, and a greater focus on intra-organizational policy and training around ethical data practices.

If there is a goal to this "playbook," it is this: the creation of the political will to corral data practices into something that forms a more perfect union, establishes justice, ensures domestic tranquility, provides for the common defense, promotes the general welfare, and sustains the blessings of liberty for ourselves and our posterity.

— *The End* —

Glossary

Accountability: In data ethics, the characteristic of an organization or program that provides for oversight of, final decision making for, and justification of data collection, sharing, use, and retention practices.

Aggregated data: Data from one or more original data sources combined to increase the value of the data for a research project or analytical question; to be analytically valid, must preserve the provenance of the original data sources and the lineage of the aggregated dataset.

Anonymized data: Data that originally contained personally identifiable information, but which has been processed to remove any indicators or variables that could positively identify an individual person. There are multiple technical methodologies that could be used to anonymize data.

Big data: Data collections or datasets that are too large, too complex, or both, to be understood and assessed without using technological methodologies and applications.

Biometric data: A subset of personally identifiable data consisting of a person's physical or physiological attributes; typically refers to unique information and largely unchangeable information like a facial scan, retina scan, fingerprint, or DNA.

Business associate agreement: In the context of the Health Insurance Portability and Accountability Act (HIPAA), the contract between a healthcare provider (who is a HIPAA covered entity) and a service provider or vendor (who is not a HIPAA covered entity) that lays out the requirements and expectations of each party, principally with regard to the access, transmission, and use of protected health information (PHI) (see also Covered entity).

Business glossary: A list of data-related terms and roles and their definitions as employed by the organization in its data practices; should be an enterprise-wide document, but specific terms and definitions may vary from organization to organization.

Chief Data Officer (CDO): A C-suite role in an organization with accountability for the organization's data assets, including policies and processes addressing the full data lifecycle; separate from and equal in authority to the organization's Chief Information Officer (CIO).

Covered entity: An entity required to adhere to the rules laid out in a given piece of legislation; typically defined based on organizational characteristics (such as type or size of a business); for example, a healthcare provider as defined in HIPAA is a HIPAA covered entity.

Data broker: A company that gathers and aggregates data from original sources, packages it, and sells or licenses it to other organizations for profit; data brokers typically have no relationship or interaction with the subjects of their data collection.

Data collection: In data ethics, the process of gathering information on people, policies, operations, or topics for assessment, analysis, and decision-making; the specific target of research is sometimes not identified at the time the data is collected.

Data culture: The underlying beliefs and practices of an organization surrounding the collection, sharing, use, and retention of data; including the value an organization places on data, how an organization collects and uses data, the resources applied to ensuring a data literate workforce, and the ethical considerations internalized by the workforce.

Data curation: A discipline focused on the ongoing documentation of contextual metadata, data categorization, and data cataloging that then enables data discovery and retrieval, maintains data quality, adds value, and provides for appropriate reuse over time.

Data ethics: A branch of ethics that evaluates data practices with the potential to adversely impact people and society – in data collection, sharing and use (Open Data Institute).

Data governance: The ongoing exercise of authority and control over an organization's data assets by an identified accountable party or parties.

Data governance council: A group of senior-level officials representing various organizational interests in the data assets of the organization; accountable for ensuring consistent creation and implementation of data policies and practices; typically chaired by the organization's Chief Data Officer and including the Chief Information Officer, General Counsel, Privacy and Civil Liberties Officer (if the organization has one), key data stewards from operational subcomponents, and sometimes representation from the budget and finance area.

Data quality: The attributes of a dataset that correspond to the articulated business, mission, and/or analytical requirements for the data to be useful; is often contextual in that some organizations and use cases will prioritize different attributes. For example, it might be more important that data be "timely" and "precise" over data than "consistent" and "easy to understand;" (see also fit for use).

Data retention: In data ethics, the period of time that data must be stored and maintained by an organization for the purposes of running the organization or carrying out its mission. Data should either be archived or disposed of after the retention period has expired.

Data sharing: In data ethics, the process of making collected data available to recipients (other than the original collector of the data) for business, mission, or analytical purposes.

Data sharing agreement: A written, formal arrangement between data providers and data recipients that lays out expectations, roles, responsibilities, and limitations on the access to, processing of uses, sharing, and storage of data applicable to both parties of the agreement.

Data steward: A data governance role that has the greatest day-to-day interaction with organizational datasets; communicates and enforces legal, regulatory, and ethical requirements; and provides input to data standards, security, and access control protocols.

Data trustee: A third-party (not the collector or user of data) that acts as the accountable party for the security and integrity of data assets and who advocates for leveraging data for the benefit of the organizational mission as a whole rather than for one particular subcomponent.

Data use: In data ethics, the process of leveraging data for an articulated business, mission, or analytical purpose.

Derivative classification authority: A delegated authority from an organization's original classifier that includes incorporating, paraphrasing, restating, or generating in new form information that is already classified, and marking the newly developed material consistent with the classification markings that apply to the source information; also includes marking information based upon classification guidance from the original classifier (Executive Order 13526).

Derived data product: A dataset produced from the processing, normalization, modeling, and/or aggregation of original raw data; generally created to prepare data for a specific use case or analytical research project.

Digital transformation: Organizational adoption of technological tools and methodologies to modernize processes, improve efficiency, and/or drive innovation.

Electronic record-keeping platform: Technology that collects and organizes business or mission-critical data to facilitate discovery, retrieval, use, and disposition.

Ethical ecosystem: A data processing and use environment in which dignity, autonomy, and privacy are incorporated into every stage of the development and implementation of data tools and applications. (DMBoK; EDPS)

Executive Order: A policy document, signed by the President of the United States, which is not a congressionally-passed law, but which has the force of law specifically for U.S. Federal Executive Branch agencies and departments.

Fit for intent: In data management and data analytics, the characteristic of a dataset that describes the degree to which the collection, sharing, use, and retention of data meets articulated ethical criteria that consider transparency, privacy, accountability, and analytical rigor; an example would be a dataset of registered voters and contact information that was used to determine whether there were sufficient polling locations in the jurisdiction to avoid long lines on election day.

Fit for purpose: In data management and data analytics, the characteristic of a dataset that describes the degree to which the data, as described and assessed, is relevant to contributing to an answer to a business, mission, or research question and can be appropriately used for that analytical purpose. An example would be a dataset of registered voters and contact information, which would be "fit for purpose" in planning a political poll.

Fit for use: In data management and data analytics, the characteristic of a dataset that describes the degree to which the quality dimensions of the data create the likelihood that analytical results based on the data will be accurate and reliable in answering a business, mission, or analytical question; an example would be a dataset of registered voters and contact information which is ten years old, which may not be "fit for use" due to the lack of timeliness and accuracy of the data.

Freedom of Information Laws: Laws that give citizens and residents the right to request and receive information about the operation of their government; exist in many countries and at multiple levels of government (national, state, municipal); typically include some number of exemptions to the release of information.

Genetic data: A subset of biometric data that refers to a person's inherited biological or physiological characteristics. An example would be DNA data on a specific individual.

Informed consent: In data ethics, the permission given by an individual for collection, sharing, and use of data based upon sufficient knowledge of the data being collected, as well as the risks and benefits of providing positive approval for the sharing and use of that data.

Learning management system: Technology that facilitates the delivery, documentation, and tracking of educational or training courses; also manages full curriculum development and delivery, as well as learning plans for individual students.

Metadata: Contextual information about a dataset needed to facilitate the flow of data and enable the discovery and use of data by a defined set of users.

National security information: Information (generally related to defense or foreign policy) that has been determined under Executive Order authority to be protected from unauthorized disclosure to maintain or advance the values and fundamental interests of the country.

Need to know: A determination that a prospective recipient requires access to specific classified information in order to perform or assist in a lawful and authorized governmental function (Executive Order 13526); onus is generally on the recipient to demonstrate or justify their "need to know."

Notice and consent: A requirement that private individuals be notified of an organization's intent to collect data about them and provide affirmative consent for such collection; in a big data environment, notice and consent does not imply or require "informed consent" (see also Informed Consent).

Official records laws: Laws that require the government to document and preserve information about the operations of the government; often require agencies and departments to have a formal records management program; exist in many countries and at multiple levels of government (national, state, municipal).

Original classification authority: An individual authorized in writing, either by the President, the Vice President, or by agency heads or other officials designated by the President, to classify information in the first instance (Executive Order 13526).

Overclassification: The tendency of derivative classification authorities to classify information at a higher level than is necessary as a risk avoidance measure (see also Derivative Classification Authority).

Personally Identifiable Information (PII): Data that allows a user to positively identify or reasonably infer the identity of an individual person. Examples of personally identifiable information include, but are not limited to, unique identifiers such as Social Security Number, Driver's License Number, or

Passport Number, as well as information in combination such as full name, date of birth, and mother's maiden name.

Post-hoc analysis: Analysis conducted on data after the data has already been seen; the goal of "providing for the reuse of data" is—by definition—post hoc analysis; consideration of the potential biases in post hoc analysis is required or statistical analyses cannot be considered valid.

Privacy: In data ethics, the characteristic of an organization or a program that both protect personally identifiable information from disclosure and ensures that the organization's own use of personally identifiable information prioritizes the subject's right to be secure in their persons and effects (both physical and psychological) (see also Personally Identifiable Information).

Protected Health Information (PHI): Individually identifiable information relating to the health of or healthcare services provided to an individual that is created, collected, or transmitted, or maintained by a HIPAA-covered entity (HIPAA).

Preservation: In data analytics and data ethics, the maintenance through archiving of datasets (with accompanying contextual metadata) that have either been used to produce analytical results (providing for the ability to replicate results later) and/or have an intrinsic historical or operational value to the organization.

Proprietary data: Data created or acquired by an organization that constitutes a trade secret and/or gives the organization a competitive advantage over others in the industry or business area; includes, but is not limited to intellectual property, financial data, and client lists.

Proxy data: Data that are not directly related to the research question but are assessed to be germane to the variable being measured and used to impute relevant results; an example would be the use of zip code data on trends of loan default in an area as a determinant in the likelihood that an individual person will repay a loan.

Public good: In data ethics, the characteristic of a democratic society that fulfills the social contract between societal members and for which the government is responsible for maintaining and maximizing for the benefit of all; related to but distinct from the economic definition of "a public good" meaning a good or service provided to or accessed by the whole population with prejudice on ability to pay.

Records retention schedule: A list of types or categories of data that an organization holds, along with the length of time the organization needs to keep it to address business or mission needs, as well as what will be done with the data when it reaches the end of its useful life and the accountable party for ensuring that the instructions are carried out.

Responsibility to share: A philosophy of intelligence sharing that posits that the default position of the collector of information should be to make that information as widely available as possible within the community of persons with appropriate security clearances, and that withholding of information within that community should be justified; compare to "need to know" which defaults to a justification for access, rather than a justification for withholding (see also Need To Know).

Social rights: The rights of people to achieve adequate food, adequate housing, education, health, social security, water, and sanitation, and to take part in cultural life, and to work (United Nations High Commissioner for Human Rights).

Subgroup data: A dataset formed by the breakdown of a population into a subset of participants based upon shared characteristics.

State's interest: A compelling government or public interest that overrides the specific right of an individual; an example would be a requirement that a doctor must have a license in a particular state to practice medicine there; such a requirement restricts the individual's right to engage in commerce but is upheld due to the compelling government interest in protecting the population.

Surveillance technologies: Tools and applications designed primarily to gather information on the activities and attributes of people; collection is often initially done in bulk and indiscriminately (and later mined) but can be targeted to specific individuals.

Telehealth platform: Platforms or applications designed to facilitate virtual conversations between healthcare providers and patients instead of or in addition to traditional office visits; typically are not HIPAA-covered entities (see also Covered Entity and Business Associate Agreement).

Transparency: In data ethics, the characteristic of an organization or program that makes available for public review and comment as much data as possible, including—at the very least—the data that is required for reasonable people to make an informed decision about policies and practices that impact them and impact society as a whole.

Index

www.ingramcontent.com/pod-product-compliance
Lightning Source LLC
Chambersburg PA
CBHW071416210326
41597CB00020B/3531